5-Minute Sports Devotions for Young Athletes

Build Mental Toughness, Grit, and Faith Through Biblical Wisdom

Welcome Aboard, Check Out This Limited-Time Free Bonus!

Ahoy, reader! Welcome to the Ahoy Publications family, and thanks for snagging a copy of this book! Since you've chosen to join us on this journey, we'd like to offer you something special.

Check out the link below for a FREE e-book filled with delightful facts about American History.

But that's not all - you'll also have access to our exclusive email list with even more free e-books and insider knowledge. Well, what are ye waiting for? Click the link below to join and set sail toward exciting adventures in American History.

Access your bonus here

https://ahoypublications.com/

Or, Scan the QR code!

Table of Contents

Introduction

Sports can bring out some of your best moments. A good play can lift your whole team. A tough practice can show you how strong you are.

Sports can also test you. You face pressure, mistakes, tired legs, early mornings, and long seasons. Some days you feel confident. Other days you wonder if you have what it takes.

This book is built to steady you through all of it.

There are **fifty-two devotions here, one for every week of the year**. Each one is short enough to read before school, during a break, or before a game. Every chapter centers on a single Bible verse. That verse will guide your thoughts and give you something solid to hold onto as you train, compete, and grow.

Many athletes work hard on their bodies. Some work on their skills, but the strongest athletes also train their hearts and minds. They know that attitude, choices, and faith matter. You may win or lose on any given day, but you can still grow in mental toughness, grit, and faith.

Think of these pages as a steady voice in your corner. You'll find reminders to stay calm under pressure, listen well, push through challenges, serve your team, and trust God when you feel unsure. You'll read about people in Scripture who had to face fear, wait for answers, handle conflict, or keep going when nothing seemed easy. They learned to rely on God, and you can do the same.

You don't need perfect talent for God to use you. You only need a willing heart.

Here's something else to remember: none of this is about being famous or impressive. It's about learning to honor God in small choices, quiet routines, and steady effort. Whether you play a full game or sit on the bench, you can show character. Whether you win a medal or not, you can show faith. God sees every moment.

As you begin, know this: these fifty-two devotions were written to move with you across the year, week by week, helping your heart grow stronger, calmer, and more confident in the Lord. Whatever sport you love, and whatever season you're in, God is with you. He knows your steps. He strengthens you, and He cares about how you play, how you train, and how you treat others.

Now, let's get started.

PART I
Heart Set:
Building a Strong Inner Life

Chapter 1

"Have I not commanded you? Be strong and courageous. Do not be afraid; do not be discouraged, for the Lord your God is with you wherever you go." - Joshua 1:9

Strength may look simple when you watch your favorite athletes on TV. They move with confidence. They seem to handle pressure well. They step into big moments with calm hearts.

Remember this: every strong athlete you admire has felt fear. Every confident player has faced doubt. Every skilled leader has worried they might fail. Strength is not the absence of fear. It is choosing courage even when fear is loud.

This verse from Joshua tells the story of a young leader stepping into a huge role. He had followed Moses for years. Moses was strong, wise, and respected. Now Joshua had to lead the entire nation. He had to face new challenges. He had to guide people who looked up to him.

He had to do this while stepping into battles he had never fought before. God knew Joshua felt unsure. God knew the task felt huge. So God gave him clear words. *Be strong. Be courageous. Do not be afraid. Do not be discouraged. I am with you.*

These words fit athletes today more than you may realize.

Every time you step into a game or practice, something inside you is learning strength. Not just physical strength, but heart strength, steady courage that comes from trusting God.

You may face a formidable opponent. You may face a coach who expects a lot from you. You may face a moment where you must take the shot, step to the line, or stand in the spotlight. In all of these moments, fear tries to speak. Fear tells you that you might mess up. Fear tells you that others are better. Fear tells you that you are unprepared. But courage tells a different story. Courage says, "I can breathe. I can trust God. I can give my best today."

Courage is not loud or flashy. Many times, it is quiet. It comes from the deep confidence that God is with you. You may feel nervous, but you're not alone. You may question your ability, but God has not left you. Strength grows when you learn to say, "God, steady me. Help me give me what I have today."

Think about a time when you felt fear in your sport. Maybe you worried about disappointing your team. You might have feared making a mistake in front of a crowd. Perhaps you had to compete after a rough practice or a week when nothing seemed to go right. Those moments can shape you. They can either shrink or strengthen you. What makes the difference is what you choose to believe.

Joshua 1:9 urges you to remember two truths:

1. God commands courage.

2. God stays with you.

These two truths work together. God never commands courage without also giving support. He doesn't tell you to be strong and then walk away. He stays right beside you. On the days you feel confident, He is with you. On the days you feel unsure, He is still with you. Your strength begins with remembering this.

In sports, many young athletes think courage belongs to the strongest players. They believe only the best competitors are brave.

Remember: Courage is not something only "elite" players get. Courage is something God builds into anyone who trusts Him. Courage grows in regular days, during quiet workouts, early mornings, long drills, or tiring scrimmages. It grows each time you practice through discomfort, each time you bounce back from a mistake, each time you choose effort even when you feel worn out.

Courage also grows through small decisions. Choosing to try again after a bad play is courage. Choosing to push through the final minute of a drill is courage. Choosing to speak kindly during a tense moment is courage. Choosing to listen to correction rather than react is courage. Courage in sports is a collection of steady choices.

Joshua had to step into an unknown future. You step into your own version of that each time you compete. You don't know how the game will end. You don't know how you will play. You don't know how others will respond.

God's presence gives you the grounding you need. You can walk into any situation with a calm heart when you trust that God is with you.

Fear often grows in silence. When you keep it inside, fear feels bigger. Part of courage is talking to God about what worries you. Say, "Lord, You know what I'm afraid of. Help me trust You." That simple prayer carries strength. God cares about the details of your sport. He sees your effort. He knows your challenges. He knows what stretches you and what pressures you. He is not distant. He is close.

Strength also grows when you remember who you are playing for. Many athletes place their identity in their performance. A good game makes them feel valuable. A bad game makes them feel small.

Your value doesn't rise or fall based on points, minutes, or stats. Your value comes from God. He made you. He sees your heart. He calls you loved and chosen. That truth frees you from fear. When your identity is safe, pressure loses some of its weight.

Courage also means being willing to grow. You won't be perfect, no athlete is. You will miss shots, lose races, misjudge plays, or misunderstand instructions. Courage says, "I can learn. I can get better. I can keep going." This keeps you from giving up when things feel hard. It builds grit over time.

Think of a sport you love. Think of a moment you felt nervous. Then imagine God speaking the same words He spoke to Joshua. *Be strong. Be courageous. Do not be afraid. Do not be discouraged. I am with you.* Those words were true then. They are true now.

The next time you face a tough moment in practice or a game, pause for a quiet second. Take a breath. Tell yourself, "God is with me right now." That simple thought can calm your heart and sharpen your focus. Strength grows when you remember you're not alone.

As you move through this week, try this: before each practice or game, repeat Joshua 1:9 quietly. Let it settle in your mind. Let it shape the way you face pressure. You are not asked to be perfect. You are asked to be steady. To be courageous. To be faithful. God supplies the strength you need.

Courage is a choice you can make each day. God will meet you there.

Chapter 2

"The Lord is my strength and my shield; my heart trusts in him, and he helps me. My heart leaps for joy, and with my song I praise him.." - Psalm 28:7

There are days when strength comes easily. You wake up feeling sharp. Your legs feel quick. Your mind feels clear. Even tough drills don't shake you. You step into practice with a kind of natural energy, and everything seems to move the way you hoped.

There are other days, too, when you feel heavier the moment you open your eyes. Days when your body feels slow. Days when mistakes come faster than good moments, and nothing seems to click. Days when you can't explain the tight feeling in your chest, or you wonder why your confidence feels far away.

Psalm 28:7 says strength comes from the Lord.

That means your strength is not limited to how you feel in the moment. It isn't tied to your mood, or energy level, or whether you had a good game last week.

It comes from Someone steady, Someone who doesn't get tired, Someone who doesn't lose focus, Someone who never wakes up drained or discouraged.

When God becomes your strength, you stop relying on your emotions to decide what kind of day you will have. You learn to trust a source that doesn't run out.

This verse also calls God your **shield**. A shield doesn't remove the fight; it protects you in the middle of it. For athletes, the battles aren't always physical. They show up in your thoughts: pressure, fear, comparison, doubt. They show up in disappointment, in overthinking, in frustration after a mistake. They show up in the silent moments on the bench or the long walk to the locker room.

A shield goes where you go. It stays between you and the things that try to break your spirit. When Scripture calls God your shield, it doesn't mean He blocks all hard things. It means He stands in front of you during them. You don't take the full hit. You don't fight alone. You don't face pressure without His covering.

Notice how the verse continues: *"My heart trusts in Him, and He helps me."*

Trust comes before help. Not because God refuses to help without it, but because trust opens your heart enough to notice His presence.

When you trust God, your mindset shifts.

You stop panicking when things go wrong.

You stop assuming every mistake ruins everything.

You stop believing your value changes based on your performance.

Trust steadies you. It gives you the courage to breathe even when your chest feels tight. It helps you step back into the game after a rough moment. It stops your thoughts from spinning out of control. Trust is not pretending everything is fine. Trust is remembering that God is with you, even when nothing feels fine.

Then, something beautiful happens: *"My heart leaps for joy."*

Joy, not as loud excitement or hype, but as a quiet, steady confidence.

Joy that comes from knowing you're held.

Joy that comes from knowing you're supported.

Joy that comes from knowing you don't have to be perfect to be loved.

Joy that isn't tied to circumstances but to God's presence.

Athletes often chase joy in the wrong places: approval, achievements, recognition, roles, highlights. Those things feel good for a moment, but they fade quickly. Joy that comes from the Lord lasts. It settles in you. It carries you through ups and downs. It gives you strength when excitement is gone.

Joy and strength go hand in hand. When your heart is joyful, your steps feel lighter. When your spirit is weighed down, even simple tasks feel harder. God knows this, which is why He doesn't only strengthen you: He restores joy to you.

Think about a time when a small encouragement changed your whole day.

A teammate said something kind.

A coach noticed your effort.

A parent hugged you at the right moment.

You made one good play that reminded you of your ability.

Those moments lifted you because joy has power. Now imagine the joy God gives: quiet, deep, steady, not dependent on performance. That joy doesn't rise and fall. It sits in your chest like a warm light that reminds you: *I am not alone. I am not forgotten. I am loved. I am strengthened.*

There will be days when you forget this. Days when frustration clouds everything. Days when trust feels harder than usual. Days when joy feels distant. On those days, return to this verse. Read it slowly. Let each word settle:

The Lord is my strength.

The Lord is my shield.

My heart trusts Him.

He helps me.

My heart leaps for joy.

This isn't a motivational quote. It's a truth spoken over your life by God Himself.

Before your next game or practice, try this simple act: place your hand over your heart and whisper, "Lord, be my strength and my shield today."

Not long. Not fancy. Just honest.

You may notice your breathing slow.

You may feel tension leave your shoulders.

You may feel courage rise where fear usually sits.

Even if you feel nothing at all, trust that God is already working in you.

You don't have to create strength by yourself.

You don't have to protect your heart alone.

You don't have to carry pressure without help.

You have a God who strengthens you, shields you, helps you, and fills your heart with joy that outlasts every challenge ahead.

Walk into today knowing that the same God who gave strength to David, courage to Joshua, peace to Daniel, and joy to Paul is with you: right now, right here, in your season, in your sport, in your life.

He will not fail you.

Chapter 3

"Above all else, guard your heart, for everything you do flows from it." -
Proverbs 4:23

Your heart is at the center of everything you do. It shapes your attitude, choices, focus, and even your approach to competition. When this verse advises you to "guard your heart," it's not suggesting that you build walls or shut people out. Instead, it means paying attention to what you allow to enter your heart. It involves protecting the thoughts, habits, and influences that shape the way you live and play.

Imagine you have a water bottle you rely on during practice. You keep it clean because you know that whatever is inside it is going into your body. You wouldn't let dirt, mud, or trash fall into it. You would keep it sealed when you're not using it. You would check it often. You guard it because you need it.

Your heart works similarly. It is the well of your life. Whatever fills it, good or bad, eventually shows up in your words, your reactions, your effort, and your relationships. That is why this verse calls your heart something to protect with intention.

Young athletes face many influences. Some help you grow. Some push you away from who God calls you to be. You hear voices from friends, teammates, coaches, parents, teachers, and social media. You may not notice it at first, but those voices can shape how you think and feel. You may find confidence or doubt. Hope or frustration. Grit or discouragement. Peace or chaos.

Guarding your heart means asking, "Is this helping me follow God? Is this helping me grow stronger inside? Or is this pushing me toward worry, anger, or insecurity?"

Think about the last time you felt weighed down after practice. Maybe someone criticized you in a hurtful way. Maybe you compared yourself to someone else and felt small. It could be that you kept replaying a mistake in your mind. These moments show exactly why your heart needs protection. If you let these thoughts sit unchecked, they create cracks. They drain your joy. They shake your confidence.

Guarding your heart starts with awareness. Pay attention to the things that weaken you inside. Notice what drains your energy. Notice what stirs frustration or fear. Notice what steals your focus. When you see these things, bring them to God. He is the one who strengthens and cleans your heart.

Some athletes think guarding your heart means being tough all the time.

Remember: Guarding your heart is about choosing what guides you. You can be honest about your feelings and still protect your heart. You can acknowledge a hard moment without letting it define you.

For example, imagine you had a rough game. Instead of saying, "I'm terrible. I'll never get better," you can choose a guarded response: "That was a tough game, but I can learn from it. God is still with me." This response does not deny the truth, but it keeps your heart safe. It keeps you grounded in God's care.

Protecting your heart also means guarding what you listen to. People may speak out of frustration, stress, or lack of understanding. Not every voice deserves space inside your heart. Learn to filter what you hear. When a coach corrects you, receive it with humility. When a teammate encourages you, let it help you.

When someone tries to tear you down or speak negatively about your life, bring that straight to God and refuse to let it take root.

You will hear opinions about your performance. Some will help you. Some will distract you. Guard your heart by remembering this: your worth is not defined by talent, stats, or the approval of others. Your worth comes from the One who made you and calls you His child.

Guarding your heart also means protecting your attitude. Your attitude can shift fast in sports. One moment, you feel locked in. The next moment a bad call, a missed shot, or a tough drill can turn your heart sour. This is normal, but it is also a space where you can grow.

When frustration rises, pause. Take one slow breath. Steady your mind. Tell yourself, "Lord, guard my heart right now." This small step gives you space to respond instead of react. It helps you choose patience over anger, effort over quitting, and composure over panic.

Some athletes lose their joy because they forget to guard their hearts against jealousy. You see a teammate improving fast. You see someone getting more playing time. You see another athlete getting praise. If you're not careful, jealousy can settle in your heart like a slow leak. It drains energy and kills unity.

The best way to guard against jealousy is gratitude. Thank God for your gifts. Thank God for another player's gifts. Thank God for the chance to grow alongside them. Gratitude keeps your heart open, healthy, and steady.

Guarding your heart also involves your private thoughts, what you think about during quiet moments.

Many battles in sports are fought inside your mind. When negative thoughts show up, "I can't do this," "I always mess up," "Everyone is ahead of me," bring them into the light. Replace them with truth. Say, "God is with me," "I am growing," or "I can keep going because God strengthens me."

God never asks you to pretend. He does ask you to protect the place where your choices begin.

Another part of guarding your heart is guarding what you see. Social media can weaken your heart if you use it without care. You may scroll through highlight plays and compare yourself to people you've never met. You may see comments that stir anxiety. You may see athletes who seem perfect and start to feel inadequate. Guard your heart by limiting what pulls you toward insecurity. Focus on real-life growth instead of online images that may not be real.

Guarding your heart also means guarding your relationships. The people you spend time with shape your mindset. Choose teammates and friends who build you up, not those who pull you into trouble or negativity. You do not have to shut people out, but you should be wise about who influences you the most.

When your heart is guarded, everything else flows better. Your effort grows. Your focus sharpens. Your emotions settle. Your decisions become wiser. Your reactions become steadier. You compete with purpose instead of pressure.

God cares about your heart more than your skills. Skills can be trained. Strength can be built. Speed can improve.

Your heart is the core of who you are. When your heart is healthy, everything else works a lot more smoothly.

As you step into this week, take a moment before practice or school and pray, "Lord, guard my heart today." Ask Him to help you recognize the things that pull you down. Ask Him to show you what strengthens you. Ask Him to steady your attitude and your thoughts. Ask Him to keep His truth at the center of everything you do.

Your heart guides your life, and God stands ready to protect it. When your heart is guarded, you become the kind of athlete who is calm under pressure, steady in adversity, faithful in growth, and strong from the inside out.

Let God shape and guard your heart, and everything else will follow.

Chapter 4

"Therefore, since we are surrounded by such a great cloud of witnesses, let us throw off everything that hinders and the sin that so easily entangles. And let us run with perseverance the race marked out for us." - Hebrews 12:1

Endurance is a quality that every athlete desires, but few enjoy developing.

It requires more than strength; it demands consistent effort, even when the initial excitement fades. Building endurance involves pushing through fatigue and holding focus even when the mind wants to give up. It means continuing to move forward even when progress feels slow. Endurance grows during those quiet moments when you choose to persevere.

The writer of Hebrews uses the image of a race to explain endurance. Not a quick sprint. Not a sudden burst of energy. A race that takes time, focus, and patience. For many young athletes, this idea fits well. Your season isn't one day. Your growth isn't one drill. Your training requires commitment over weeks, months, and sometimes years.

When the verse says "the race that is set before us," it means the race God has given *you*. Not someone else's race. Not the path another athlete is taking. Not the timeline or pace you see online. Your race has its own challenges, its own victories, and its own slow days.

When you compare your path to someone else's, endurance becomes harder. You start to feel behind. You question your progress. You doubt your place.

When you focus on the path God placed in front of you, you can run with more peace and clarity.

Endurance in your sport begins with accepting where you are. You may want to be faster, stronger, or more skilled. You may want more playing time or better results. Those goals are good, but endurance calls you to stay faithful in the stage you're in right now. Improvement comes through small steps. Some days feel great. Some days feel tough. Every day matters.

Think about your toughest practice. Maybe your legs felt heavy. Maybe drills seemed endless. Perhaps your coach pushed you harder than usual. You reached a point where you thought about stopping, but something inside you kept moving. Even small steps count. That moment, when you continue despite discomfort, is where endurance grows.

Endurance is built in layers. First, you push through physical tiredness. Then, you push through mental doubt. Last, you push through emotional discouragement. Every layer matters. Every layer teaches you something about yourself and about God.

Physical endurance teaches you discipline. Your body learns that it can go farther than your mind first thought. You learn the difference between giving up and resting. You learn how to pace yourself. You learn that consistency matters more than sudden bursts of effort.

Mental endurance teaches you how to handle thoughts. During long runs or tough drills, your mind may say, "I can't keep going."

Then, you take another step. Each step proves your mind wrong. Over time, you learn to filter your thoughts. You learn that you don't have to obey every negative idea that crosses your mind. You learn how to stay focused when distractions show up.

Emotional endurance teaches you how to deal with frustration, fear, or disappointment. You learn how to keep your heart steady even when things don't go your way. You learn how to bounce back after mistakes. You learn to trust God more deeply because you experience His strength working through your weakness.

The verse also reminds us that endurance grows when we remove what slows us down. In sports, that may look like letting go of bad habits, distractions, or attitudes that weigh you down. It may mean limiting time with people who discourage you. It may mean choosing better routines. It may mean stepping back from things that drain your focus.

In your spiritual race, this also means letting go of sin, unhealthy influences, or negative patterns. These things may not seem heavy at first, but they can slow you down over time. God calls you to run freely, with nothing pulling you off course.

Endurance also grows when you remember that you are not running alone. The verse uses the word "us." You are part of a community. In sports, you have teammates. You train together. You suffer through drills together. You celebrate wins together. In faith, you also have people who run with you: family, friends, mentors, and believers who encourage you.

Even more important, Jesus ran the race before you. He knows what pressure feels like. He knows what exhaustion feels like. He knows what it means to struggle, to be misunderstood, to face difficulty, and to push through hard moments. When you feel worn out, remember that Jesus understands. His strength can meet you right where you feel weak.

Think about a race where someone is cheering for you. Their voice gives you a boost. It lifts your effort. It helps you push through the final stretch. In your race of faith, God cheers for you with His presence, His Word, and His promises. He does not stand far away. He stands close, ready to help you endure.

Some athletes struggle because they expect progress to show up fast. When they don't see quick results, they think something is wrong.

Endurance grows in quiet, hidden places. It grows in the mornings when you show up for practice, even though you're tired. It grows in the moments when you choose effort over excuses. It grows when you try again after a rough day. Many people quit too early. Endurance means choosing to stay the course, even when results are slow.

One of the best ways to grow endurance is to set simple goals. Instead of saying, "I need to be perfect," say, "I will give consistent effort today." Instead of saying, "I need to be the best," say, "I will improve one small thing today." These small goals add up. They help you stay focused without overwhelming you.

Endurance also comes from learning to breathe through the hard moments. Many athletes hold their breath when stressed, but steady breathing calms your brain, sharpens your thinking, and helps you stay present. You can practice this even outside sports. When school feels stressful or life feels heavy, take one slow breath and say, "Lord, help me keep going."

God loves to strengthen those who feel weak. You do not have to pretend you have endless energy. You do not have to force yourself to be tough all the time. You can admit when you feel worn out. You can admit when things feel difficult. God meets you with gentleness in those moments. He strengthens you step by step.

Endurance is about running faithfully.

As you move through this week, think about your own race. Where do you feel tired? Where do you feel stretched? Where do you feel discouraged? Bring those places to God. Ask Him for strength. Ask Him for patience. Ask Him to remind you that your race matters and that you are not running alone.

Before your next practice, whisper this verse to yourself: "Let us run with endurance the race that is set before us." Let it settle in your heart. Let it shape your mindset. Let it remind you that every step counts.

Keep running. Keep growing. Keep trusting God with your race. He will give you the endurance you need.

Chapter 5

"Let us not become weary in doing good, for at the proper time we will reap a harvest if we do not give up." - Galatians 6:9

Some days in sports feel long, really long. You show up with good intentions, but your body feels heavy. You miss your passes. Your shots don't make it. Your coach pushes you to do better, and you want to, but deep down, you feel worn out. It's more than being tired. It's that heavy feeling that makes you question if all the effort matters.

This verse is God's answer to moments like that.

The people who first heard these words lived in a world full of hard choices. They were trying to follow Christ, serve others, and stay faithful in a season that didn't always feel fair. They poured their hearts into "doing good," but the results took time. They didn't see quick change. Some probably wondered why God wasn't moving faster. They needed encouragement, and this verse gave it to them: *don't quit doing what is right; God sees everything, and your hard work will not disappear into the air.*

That message fits athletes today. It's quite possible you're the one who always pushes during drills, yet nobody seems to notice. Maybe you go out of your way to support teammates, but you rarely hear a "thank you."

Maybe you try to keep a good attitude when others complain, but it feels like you're carrying the team's energy all on your own. After a while, those things could make anyone feel worn down.

God knows that feeling. He knows you get tired. He knows that trying to do the right thing can feel lonely. That's why He promises something simple but powerful: **your effort matters, and none of it is wasted.**

Consider how real growth happens. When you plant a seed, you don't get a full tree overnight. First, things happen out of sight. The seed splits, roots grow, and the soil moves. It's not exciting to watch, and you can't see it from above, but something steady and alive is taking place.

Your growth as an athlete, and even more as a follower of Christ, works the same way. You train, listen, and push through tough days. You try to keep your heart steady and be patient. You choose to treat others well and honor God in small ways. At first, it might seem like nothing is changing, but God sees the roots forming. He notices the slow work happening beneath the surface.

He promises a harvest in the right season.

This "harvest" won't always look like a trophy, a starting spot, or perfect stats. Sometimes the harvest is a strength you didn't have before. Sometimes it's calmness under pressure. Sometimes it's clearer judgment, or steadier habits, or deeper character. Sometimes the harvest isn't something you hold, it's something you've become.

Let's talk about sports for a moment.

You know how tough certain phases of training can be. You run the same drill again and again. You watch films. You repeat movements until your muscles ache. None of those moments feel exciting, but those unexciting days probably do more for your future than the easy days. When you stick with the process, even when you feel weary, something in you is being shaped.

That is part of "doing good."

Yes, treating people well matters. Yes, showing kindness matters, but doing good also includes showing up and giving honest effort even when it's not fun. It's doing the right thing simply because it's right, not because someone is watching.

Sometimes doing good means choosing to stay patient with a teammate who frustrates you. Sometimes it means stepping back after a mistake instead of lashing out. Sometimes it means cleaning up equipment when you'd rather go straight home. Sometimes it means staying calm when a game gets physical or emotions run high. These choices reveal your character long before the scoreboard does.

Here's the honest truth: doing what is right all the time can feel tiring. That's why this verse warns you about "growing weary." Weariness slowly sneaks in. It doesn't arrive with a loud announcement. It shows up in quiet ways: discouragement, frustration, impatience, or the feeling that nobody cares.

That is exactly why God tells you, "Don't give up."

He's not telling you to pretend everything is easy. He's reminding you that good work takes time. He's reminding you that your character matters more than your speed or strength. He's reminding you that He is the One keeping track of your effort, even when others overlook it.

You don't need applause to keep doing good. You don't need to be the star player to live out this verse. You just need a heart that says, "God, help me stay faithful today."

Take a moment to think back over the last few weeks. Was there a day when you felt invisible? Was there a moment when you tried to do the right thing but felt unappreciated? Was there a time when you showed kindness and got nothing in return? Those moments are not useless. They are the soil where God grows endurance, kindness, strength, and humility.

Even Jesus faced this. He healed people. He helped crowds. He taught with patience. Yet many walked away from Him. Many misunderstood Him. Still, He kept doing good because His heart was anchored in His Father. His example shows you that doing good isn't about getting something back, it's about living in a way that honors God.

So, how do you keep going when you feel worn out? One of the most helpful steps is to give God the burden. Tell Him you feel weary. Tell Him you're discouraged. Tell Him you want to stop trying. God doesn't scold you for being honest. He meets you with comfort and strength.

Another step is to remember the "why." Why do you work hard? Why do you treat people with respect? Why do you aim to honor God? When you remember your purpose, weariness loses some of its weight.

Also, take time to rest, real rest. Not scrolling on your phone, but rest that quiets your mind. Rest that lets God speak to your heart again. Rest that reminds you that you don't have to carry everything on your own.

Here's something small you can try this week: Before practice or school, say quietly, "Lord, help me not grow weary in doing good today." You don't have to shout it. You don't even have to say it out loud. Just set your heart in that direction.

Remember, God never overlooks faithfulness. Even when you feel unseen, God sees you. Even when you feel slow, God is working. Even when you feel tired, God is close.

Keep doing good. Keep trusting Him. Your harvest is on the way.

Chapter 6

"But the Lord said to Samuel, "Do not consider his appearance or his height, for I have rejected him. The Lord does not look at the things people look at. People look at the outward appearance, but the Lord looks at the heart." - 1 Samuel 16:7

Sports place a lot of attention on what people can see. Coaches watch how fast you move, how high you jump, how strong you look, and how you react under pressure. Teammates notice who takes the big shots, who has the cleanest footwork, and who seems confident. Fans watch the scoreboard. Parents watch for improvement. You may even catch yourself watching others, comparing what they can do with what you're still trying to figure out.

It's easy to feel like everything that matters in sports happens on the outside.

Scripture cuts right through that idea and reminds you of a simple truth: God sees deeper. He looks past the surface. He looks straight at your heart.

This verse comes from the story of David. Samuel had been told to find the next king. Everyone expected someone tall, strong, and impressive. They assumed leadership had a certain "look," and David didn't have it. He was the youngest son, the kid who worked in the fields while his brothers trained for battle. No one even considered him for the role. Yet God chose him, not because of his appearance, but because of his heart. David trusted God, and that mattered more than any skill his brothers had.

Many young athletes need to hear that today. Have you stood there during a tryout, hoping someone would notice you? Maybe you've watched other players get more praise or more attention, or you felt invisible even after giving everything you had. Moments like that can make you wonder whether you're falling behind or whether others see you as valuable at all.

God does, and He sees more than anyone else ever will.

He sees the quiet choices you make. He sees the days you push yourself even when you would rather stay home. He sees the effort you put into being a good teammate. He sees your patience when things don't go the way you hoped. He sees your honesty when you admit you're frustrated. He sees your desire to grow. He sees your willingness to keep trusting Him, even in disappointing seasons. When God looks at you, He sees all of this and He calls it valuable.

People can miss things. They can overlook the moments that reveal your character. They may judge quickly, or simply misunderstand you.

God sees the whole picture. Nothing good in your heart goes unnoticed by Him.

This truth can bring comfort, but it can also bring direction. If God looks at your heart, then your character matters even on the days when your performance doesn't shine. You don't need to be the fastest or the strongest to please Him. You need a heart that seeks Him. A heart that stays humble. A heart that listens. A heart that is willing to grow.

Think about a day when your performance wasn't great. Maybe you missed opportunities. Maybe your coach corrected you again and again. Maybe you were frustrated. In moments like that, your heart is tested more than your skills. Will you shut down? Will you get angry? Will you blame others? Or will you stay teachable? A teachable heart is one of the most powerful things you can bring into any sport.

A strong heart can grow even in quiet moments. When you wake up early to train, even though you don't feel like it, your heart is getting stronger. When you congratulate a teammate who beat you out for a position, your heart is getting stronger. When you listen to instructions without arguing, your heart is getting stronger. When you choose kindness over frustration, your heart is getting stronger.

God notices each of these choices, even if no one else comments on them.

A lot of athletes today feel pressure to look confident, even when they're not. They feel pressure to appear fearless. They feel pressure to act like they have everything under control.

God isn't asking you to put on a show. He isn't impressed by pretending. He responds to honesty. When you say, "Lord, I'm nervous," or "I feel overwhelmed," that honesty opens the door for Him to steady you.

A heart that seeks God doesn't need to hide weakness. Weakness is a place where God's strength grows.

Sometimes your heart gets shaken by comparison. You see someone else your age doing things you wish you could do. You hear people talking about another player's talent. You notice teammates improving faster than you. If you're not careful, comparison starts to cloud your heart. It steals joy. It whispers lies. It makes you think you're not enough.

This verse reminds you that God is not comparing you to anyone. He sees your journey, your pace, your growth, and your challenges. He knows exactly what He is shaping in you. When you trust Him, you can focus on your lane instead of trying to race someone else's.

There will also be moments when you feel misunderstood. Maybe a teammate judges your quietness as a lack of effort. Maybe a coach mistakes your nerves for lack of focus. Those things hurt.

Remember: David was overlooked too. People failed to see what God saw in him. Yet, God chose him anyway.

If God sees something in you, that is enough. Let His voice weigh more than anyone else's.

A heart that pleases God doesn't lift itself above others. David wasn't prideful or selfish. He served faithfully in the small places long before he ever stepped into leadership. You can follow that same example. Look for ways to serve the people around you. Help a teammate gather equipment. Say kind words to someone who's had a rough game. Include someone who feels out of place. A heart that notices others reflects Christ in every setting, even practices.

Hard seasons also shape your heart. When you sit on the bench more than you want, your heart is tested. When you're injured and have to watch instead of compete, your heart is tested. When school stress and sports stress feel like too much, your heart is tested. It's in these moments that God often does His best work. He builds grit, patience, and maturity in you. He draws you closer to Him.

Before you head into your next practice or game, take a quiet moment to pray, "Lord, look at my heart and guide it today." That one sentence can shift your entire mindset. Instead of worrying about how you appear to others, you focus on what matters most, honoring God with who you are, not just what you do.

You don't have to impress God. You simply have to trust Him. He sees your heart clearly, and He knows what He can grow in you. When you let Him shape your heart, the rest of your life: your effort, your attitude, your reactions begins to show it.

Let that truth settle in you. God sees you. He values you. He knows you. He cares about your heart far more than the world ever will.

Chapter 7

"Create in me a pure heart, O God, and renew a steadfast spirit within me.." - Psalm *51:10*

Some days in sports go by smoothly. You play well, your mind feels clear, you connect with teammates, and you walk off the field or court with a light heart. Other days feel heavier. You might get frustrated, speak too quickly, react in a way you later regret, or carry a level of tension that follows you long after practice ends. On those days, your heart can feel cluttered, crowded with stress, disappointment, or guilt.

Psalm 51:10 is a prayer for days like that. David prayed these words after making mistakes that weighed heavily on him. He didn't try to hide. He didn't pretend he felt fine. He went straight to God and asked for a clean heart and a renewed spirit. That honesty is something every young athlete can learn from.

A pure heart doesn't mean a perfect heart. It means a heart that is open, humble, and willing to let God help clear out what doesn't belong. In sports, as in life, you build habits in your heart just as much as you build strength in your body. A pure heart helps you handle pressure with patience, treat others with respect, and bounce back from mistakes without beating yourself up.

Think about what happens to your room during a busy week. You don't mean to make a mess. It just happens: clothes on the floor, water bottles left around, papers stacking up. Then one day you walk in and think, "This space obviously needs attention." Your heart can feel like that, too. Stress piles up. Disappointments get buried within. Sharp words from someone pierce deeper than you expected. Fears take up space you didn't plan to give them. It doesn't happen all at once, but over time, you can feel the weight.

Asking God to "create a pure heart" is like pausing long enough to let Him help you reset. It's a way of saying, "Lord, I don't like how this feels. I need Your help. Clear out what's getting in the way."

Young athletes often try to push through everything without stopping to reflect. You have schoolwork, practices, games, friendships, expectations, and a schedule that rarely slows down.

When you carry too much inside, it affects your performance, your confidence, and your attitude. A clean heart brings clarity. It helps you see moments honestly instead of through frustration or fear.

A pure heart is also connected to your character. Sports constantly test your reactions. You may feel tempted to snap after a bad call, even wanting to blame someone when a play goes wrong. You may feel irritated when a teammate makes a mistake. You might even feel ashamed after losing your cool. Those reactions don't make you a bad person, but they do reveal places where your heart needs attention. God is not surprised by those moments. He knows the pressures you face. He knows competition brings out strong emotions. He invites you to bring those moments to Him.

David's prayer includes another key phrase: "renew a steadfast spirit within me." This is a steady one. A humble one. A teachable one. It's the kind of attitude that helps you stay grounded when things get tough. It helps you respond with patience instead of anger. It helps you accept corrections without falling apart. It helps you compete hard without letting pride or frustration take over.

When your spirit is steady, you can be at peace when you play. You listen and communicate better. You enjoy the sport more. You also reflect Christ more clearly to the people around you.

Let's take a moment to talk about guilt. After a tough game or a reaction you regret, it's common for athletes to feel guilty. You might replay mistakes in your mind, think about things you wish you hadn't said, or remember when you let your frustration show. Guilt can feel like a heavy weight in your heart. It can distract you and take away your joy. One way to let go of guilt is to ask God to give you a pure heart. When you confess, God doesn't shame you or hold your past against you. He forgives, heals, and restores. His goal is to set you free.

A pure heart also helps you forgive others. In sports, you'll face teammates who lose their temper, opponents who talk trash, or games filled with tension. It's easy to hold onto hurt.

Forgiveness clears space in your heart. Anger and bitterness take energy away from your growth. Forgiveness doesn't excuse what happened, but it releases you from carrying the weight.

Think about a moment when you felt frustrated with yourself or someone else. Maybe a teammate yelled at you unfairly. Maybe your coach pointed out something in a harsh tone. Maybe you let emotions get the best of you. These moments don't have to control your future. When you ask God to renew your spirit, He gives you strength to move forward with grace.

Another part of a clean heart is honesty, with yourself and others. You can tell God exactly how you feel, even the messy parts. You can say, "Lord, I'm angry," or "I'm disappointed," or "I'm embarrassed," or "I don't understand why this happened." God already knows what's inside you. Being honest allows Him to work with you. He isn't waiting for perfect words. He's waiting for an open heart.

A pure heart also makes room for good things to grow. When fear leaves, courage grows. When bitterness leaves, compassion grows. When pride leaves, humility grows. When guilt leaves, confidence grows. When frustration leaves, patience grows. God replaces the things that weigh you down with things that build you up.

Think about breathing after a hard run. When you finally catch your breath, everything feels clearer. Your vision sharpens. Your body feels lighter. Your head stops spinning. A pure heart feels like that: lighter, calmer, more focused. It doesn't remove all challenges, but it gives you a way to face them without being tangled up inside.

So, how do you make this prayer part of your life as an athlete?

Start small. Before practice, whisper, "Create in me a clean heart, Lord." When you feel frustration rising, take one slow breath and repeat it silently. When you walk off the field after a tough day, say it again. Let that prayer shape your responses and guide your thinking.

When you feel disappointed, go to God instead of hiding it. When you feel guilty, confess and let Him lift the weight. When you feel overwhelmed, ask Him to steady your spirit. When you feel unsure, ask Him to renew your courage.

Over time, this simple prayer helps build a heart that handles pressure with grace and admits weakness without fear. It teaches you to trust God with the deepest parts of yourself.

A pure heart isn't something you create on your own. It's something God shapes in you.

When your heart is cleaned and renewed, your entire life, sports included, feels clearer, steadier, and more grounded.

God wants your heart. Bring it to Him with honesty. He will renew it with strength.

Chapter 8

"I have told you these things, so that in me you may have peace. In this world you will have trouble. But take heart*! I have overcome the world." - John 16:33*

Before a big game or meet, athletes often hear phrases meant to pump them up. "You've got this." "Don't overthink it." "Just be confident." Those lines sound good, but they don't always match how you feel. Sometimes your stomach is tight. Sometimes doubt creeps in no matter how many times you tell yourself to relax. Sometimes trouble shows up in ways that feel bigger than your sport: friend issues, a rough week at school, or stress you can't quite explain. Confidence doesn't always flip on like a light switch.

That's why the words of Jesus in this verse sound different from anything else. He doesn't pretend life is easy. He doesn't give a quick pep talk. He speaks truth first: "You will have trouble."

Not "might," or, "maybe." He says trouble is part of life for everyone.

Then, He gives a command strong enough to steady anyone: "Take heart."

To "take heart" is to breathe again when fear rises. It's to choose courage when circumstances feel heavy. It's finding calm when your mind wants to roam. It's holding onto hope even when the scoreboard or the situation isn't in your favor.

Jesus doesn't leave you alone in that choice. He gives the reason you can take heart: "I have overcome the world."

For a young athlete, that truth is huge. It means your confidence doesn't depend only on how prepared you feel. It doesn't rest on perfect conditions or the approval of others. It rests on Jesus, who has already overcome every struggle life can bring.

Think about a moment in your sport when things went wrong. Maybe your team fell behind early. Maybe you tried your best and still made mistakes. Maybe someone else's attitude threw you off.

Moments like these bring pressure, and pressure often brings emotions you didn't expect: fear, frustration, embarrassment, or even sadness. These emotions don't make you weak. They make you human. Jesus knew His followers would face stress and fear, and He spoke this verse to remind them they could still find courage in Him.

Taking heart is not pretending trouble doesn't exist. It's facing trouble with a different source of strength.

Picture yourself sitting on a bench or catching your breath between plays. Everything around you feels tense. The game may be close. Perhaps you're frustrated with yourself. Maybe you feel the weight of letting others down. In that moment, taking heart looks like pausing long enough to whisper, "Lord, steady me." It's not dramatic. It's not loud. It's honest.

Trouble doesn't always come from the outside. Sometimes it comes from inside your thoughts. Maybe you battle fear of failure. Maybe you feel like everyone else is improving faster than you, and so you replay every mistake long after practice ends. Trouble can show up in silence, and no one else knows it's there. Jesus sees the problems you don't talk about. He sees the pressure you keep inside.

He calls you to take heart because He has already overcome the weight of the world, including the weight you carry.

You don't have to be fearless to take heart. You simply have to look to the One who is bigger than your fear.

Some athletes think courage is a personality trait, something loud, bold, and flashy.

Remember: courage can be quiet. A quiet kind of courage shows up when you step back into a drill after messing up. It shows up when you choose not to quit even when you feel discouraged. It shows up when you stay calm after a rough play. It shows up when you give an honest effort even on a day when your body feels heavy.

Jesus invites you to that quiet courage. Not manufactured confidence. Not mask-wearing confidence. Real courage that comes from His presence.

Maybe this week you've faced trouble you didn't expect. Maybe your playing time isn't what you hoped for. Maybe a coach's words cut deeper than they meant to. Maybe a teammate treated you unfairly. Maybe life outside of sports feels stressful. Jesus doesn't dismiss any of that. He doesn't say your trouble is "small." He says, "Take heart," because nothing you face is stronger than His victory.

When Jesus says He has "overcome the world," He is saying He has faced the hardest battles and won. He faced fear, pain, loneliness, rejection, and pressure beyond anything we can imagine. He remained faithful. That victory is not distant or symbolic. It is a real source of strength for you. His victory steadies your heart in the middle of your own trouble.

Think of a relay race. If the strongest runner anchors your team, the whole group breathes a little easier. You know that no matter how tough the race starts, the anchor can finish strong. Jesus is the anchor for your life. You don't carry the full weight of the race alone. You can run your part with confidence because the One who finishes for you has already overcome.

Sometimes taking heart also means letting go. Maybe you've been holding onto worry. Maybe you've been trying to control everything. Perhaps you've been carrying stress you were never meant to carry. Taking heart means opening your hands and saying, "Lord, this is too big for me. I trust You with it." That kind of surrender is wisdom.

Here's something important: taking heart is something you may need to do again and again. Not once. Not twice. Many times. Courage fades, and Jesus invites you to return to Him each time it does. Learning to "take heart" is part of growing in maturity.

A helpful way to practice this is to pause at certain points in your day, before school, before practice, after a tough conversation, and pray, "Jesus, help me take heart today." You may not feel different right away, but over time your heart becomes steadier. Your reactions slow down. Your worries lose some power. You start to notice the peace Jesus gives, even in pressure.

Imagine stepping into a game or practice with this mindset: "There may be trouble today, mistakes, stress, tough moments, but Jesus has overcome it all. I can take heart." That doesn't erase challenges, but it does change how you face them.

Your story will include trouble. No athlete escapes that. But your story can also include courage that grows each time you turn to Jesus. His victory is your foundation. His presence is your peace. His strength is your confidence.

So, when trouble comes, and it will, remember the words He spoke right to your heart: *Take heart.* You're not alone. The One who has overcome the world walks with you.

Chapter 9

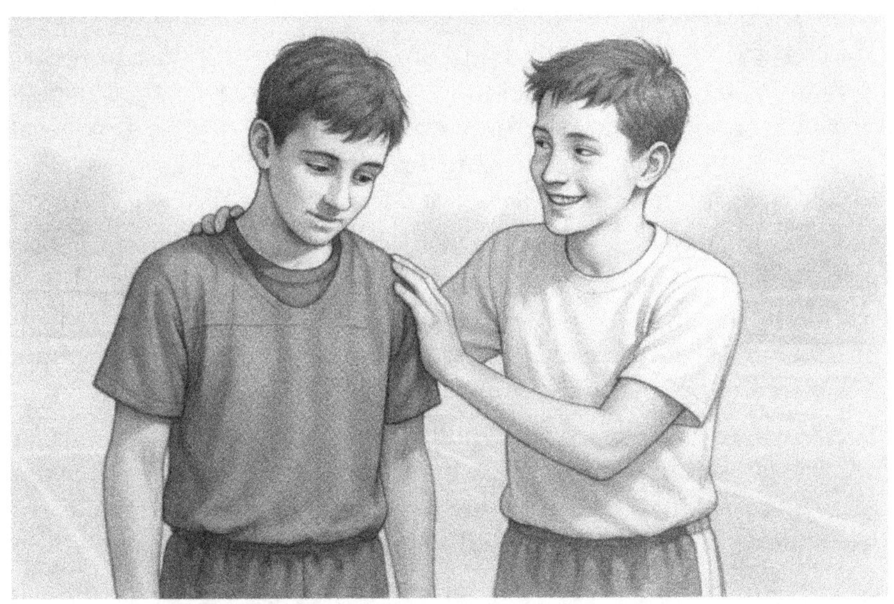

"Above all, love each other deeply, because love covers over a multitude of sins." - 1 Peter 4:8

Teams talk a lot about chemistry: trust, unity, and "playing for each other." Those things don't grow out of thin air. They grow from love. Not the mushy kind. Not the dramatic kind. Real love. The kind that shows up in quiet ways: patience, kindness, forgiveness, and a willingness to look out for someone other than yourself. This verse from 1 Peter speaks to that kind of love. It calls you to love others deeply, not halfway, not when it's convenient, but consistently and sincerely.

This kind of love sounds simple until you actually have to practice it. It's easy to love teammates on a smooth day when jokes are flying and practice is fun. It's harder when someone annoys you, or when you feel overlooked, or when a teammate blames you for something you didn't do. It's harder when you're tired, frustrated, or just want to be left alone.

Scripture doesn't say "love each other when it's easy." It says "above all else, love each other deeply."

For young athletes, this matters more than you might think. Teams rise or fall on how well players treat each other. A team full of talent but no love often collapses under pressure. They argue. They blame. They get jealous. They stop trusting each other.

A team with steady love, a team that respects each other, forgives quickly, and supports one another, can stay strong even when they don't have the biggest stars.

Think back to a moment when someone on your team encouraged you. Maybe they clapped for you after a mistake. Maybe they said your name with confidence. Maybe they shared a smile that kept you calm. That moment probably meant more to you than any big speech. Love works like that. It doesn't have to be loud to be powerful.

Now, think about a moment when someone's attitude brought the whole team down. Maybe they rolled their eyes during a drill. Maybe they yelled at someone after a turnover. Maybe they complained throughout the practice. A single person's attitude can shift an entire environment. Love can shift it too, but in the opposite direction.

Peter says love "covers over a multitude of sins." That sentence may sound strange, but it's simple: love makes room for grace. It gives space for people to mess up without getting torn down. It gives teammates room to grow. It lets you forgive instead of building bitterness.

You see this all the time in sports. A teammate misses an assignment. A pass goes the wrong direction. Someone forgets a play. Someone loses their cool. Love responds with patience, not payback. It says, "We'll get it right next time." It says, "I've messed up too. Let's keep going." Love lets people breathe.

That doesn't mean you ignore mistakes or pretend everything is perfect. It means correction delivered with respect. It means caring more about the person than the error. Love says, "Let's fix this together," not "Here's what's wrong with you."

One of the hardest parts of loving others deeply is dealing with pride. Pride whispers that you should focus on yourself. Pride says your success is the main thing. Pride tells you that someone else's good moment threatens your own. Pride pushes you to compete with teammates instead of opponents. Pride makes it hard to cheer for others.

Love has a different voice. Love celebrates when someone else shines. Love says, "Your success doesn't take anything away from me." Love builds confidence instead of tearing others down. You may not always feel that kind of love naturally, but God can grow it in you.

If you're honest, you've probably had days when you didn't feel like loving anyone. Maybe you were just too tired to show it. Maybe your patience ran out. It could even be because someone made you angry.

Love starts to feel heavy in those moments, but this verse isn't about forcing a fake smile. It's about asking God to shape your heart so that love becomes your default attitude, not your mask to wear.

One simple way to practice this is by paying attention. Notice when someone looks discouraged. Notice when someone hangs their head after a drill. Notice when someone sits alone. A quiet word, "You're doing fine," or "Shake it off, you've got this", can lift someone more than you know.

Another way to practice love is by staying calm in conflict. Sports bring conflict, whether you want it or not. Someone steps on your foot. Someone shoves you. Someone talks too much trash. Your reaction in those moments reveals what's in your heart. You might feel the urge to snap back.

Love pauses long enough to think. Love chooses restraint. Love says, "I don't have to add fuel to this fire."

Forgiveness is another part of loving deeply. Teammates hurt each other sometimes, and often by accident. Sometimes, because emotions run high. Holding grudges only blocks growth. When you forgive, your heart loosens. You breathe easier. You play freer. You walk into the next practice without a knot in your stomach.

Loving deeply also means loving the way God loves you. Think about how patient He is. Think about how many times He forgives. Think about how gently He guides you, even when you drift. When you remember how God treats you, it becomes easier to treat others with that same grace.

This kind of love strengthens teams, friendships, and families. It also strengthens you. A heart full of love handles pressure better. It reacts differently to frustration. It filters stress in a healthier way. Love gives you a bigger purpose than your stats or your spot in the lineup.

As you grow, you'll learn that people remember how you made them feel far more than they remember your performance. Years from now, teammates may not recall your best shot or your fastest run, but they will remember your kindness. They will remember how you encouraged them. They will remember how you treated them on tough days.

If you're wondering how to start loving deeply, begin small. Today, choose one teammate to encourage. Or choose one moment to stay patient instead of reacting. Or choose to apologize if you know you were harsh.

As you take small steps, love becomes part of who you are, not something you try to squeeze into your day, but something that flows naturally from your relationship with God.

Before your next practice, take ten seconds and pray, "Lord, help me love deeply today." It's a short prayer, but it sets your heart in the right direction. You may be surprised by how different your attitude feels when love leads instead of pride, fear, or frustration.

Love deeply. Love consistently. Love the way Jesus loves you. It will change your team, and it will change you.

Chapter 10

"My flesh and my heart may fail, but God is the strength of my heart and my portion forever." - Psalm 73:26

Every athlete has days when the body doesn't match the mind. Days when your legs feel heavy, your lungs feel tight, or nothing responds the way you want it to. You stretch, you warm up, you try again, but everything still feels slightly off. It's frustrating, especially when you've trained hard. You know your body is capable of more, yet for some reason, it won't cooperate.

Then there are the days when your heart feels tired too. Not the physical heart, but the emotional one. A tough day at school may wear you down. Maybe a friend lets you down. It could be that something small piles on top of something else, and before you know it, you're carrying a weight you can't quite name. When both your body and your emotions feel worn, it can be hard to stay focused, much less compete with energy.

That's what makes this verse from Psalm 73 feel so real. It doesn't hide from weakness. It doesn't pretend humans have endless strength. It says openly that your "flesh" and your "heart" may fail. They won't always hold up perfectly. They won't always deliver what you want.

Right after stating that truth, the verse gives reassurance: *God is the strength of your heart.*

For young athletes, this verse touches a place that often goes unspoken. You are expected to push, perform, rise, stay disciplined, and handle pressure with maturity. Those expectations are not wrong, but they can leave you feeling like there's no room to be human. No room to admit you're tired. No room to say, "I'm struggling today."

God already sees your weak moments, and He's not surprised by them. Weakness doesn't disappoint Him. It doesn't scare Him. It doesn't disqualify you. It simply reminds you of something important: your strength doesn't depend on you alone. God is ready to step in where your strength ends.

Consider a time when you felt worn out, not just physically but all the way to the core. Maybe you were trying to balance homework, relationships, family stress, and sports. Maybe you were pushing yourself harder than anyone knew. Perhaps you didn't want to let your team down. Maybe you felt a pressure deep inside your chest that you didn't know how to release. This verse meets you right there.

"My flesh and my heart may fail." That line gives you permission to stop pretending. It gives you permission to say, "God, I can't handle this on my own today."

Some athletes think admitting weakness means losing mental toughness. Real toughness includes honesty. It includes knowing when you need help. It includes trusting God instead of trying to carry the entire weight on your shoulders. Courage doesn't mean pushing until you break. Courage means turning to God in moments when your strength runs low.

Notice something else: the verse says God is the *strength* of your heart, not the replacement for your heart. He doesn't take away your personality, your passion, or your identity. He strengthens what's already in you. He steadies your breathing when anxiety rises. He lifts your spirit when stress weighs you down. He reminds you that your worth isn't tied to your performance.

Think about strength in a physical sense. When your legs are shaking at the end of a run, a coach or teammate's voice can give you one more burst of effort. Their encouragement becomes a kind of strength. God does something far greater. He gives strength that doesn't run out when the body does. He gives strength that reaches the parts of you that words can't touch.

There's something powerful about knowing God stays close when you're at your lowest. When you feel embarrassed after a mistake, He doesn't turn away. When you're discouraged after a rough game, He doesn't roll His eyes. When you feel overwhelmed by expectations, He doesn't add more pressure. He draws near. He supports. He steadies. He restores.

The phrase "my portion forever" means God is enough for every season, every injury, every loss, every success, every setback, every comeback. He is enough when you feel strong, and He is enough when you feel weak. Seasons change. Circumstances shift. Emotions rise and fall.

God stays constant.

Many athletes carry the idea that they have to "earn" their place. on the team, in the lineup, or in people's respect.

Your place in God's heart is not up for debate. You don't earn it by running harder or performing better. You have it because He loves you, even on the days when your strength fails.

Sometimes, the hardest battles in sports happen inside your mind. You may feel discouraged if you're not improving as fast as you hoped. You may doubt yourself after a poor performance. You may fear the future when you face injury or uncertainty. Those thoughts can drain your heart faster than any long run. That's why you need a source of strength deeper than your own ability.

Imagine going into a practice or game with this in mind: "I may not feel my best today. My body may feel weak. My emotions may be stretched, but God is the strength of my heart." That mindset doesn't deny reality. It simply adds truth to it. It says you can keep moving even when things feel heavy because your strength rests in God.

Some days, the most honest prayer you can offer is, "Lord, I'm worn out. Please hold me together today." He will. He meets humility with strength.

Here's something else to consider: God's strength often shows up in quiet ways. You might feel a sudden calm in the middle of stress. You might feel a gentle push to keep going when you thought you were done. You might find unexpected clarity in a moment that felt messy a few minutes earlier. These small moments are signs of God at work, strengthening you from the inside.

This verse also keeps you grounded in perspective. Your sport is important. Your body is important. Your heart is important. Remember: none of these define your worth. God does.

His strength isn't limited by your condition. You may feel like you're running on empty, but God's strength does not run dry.

As you move through the rest of your season, try to check in with yourself honestly. Ask, "How is my heart today?" If the answer is tired, stressed, or discouraged, bring it to God. He isn't asking for perfection. He's asking for trust.

Before you start your next practice, take a moment and breathe. Then whisper, "God, be the strength of my heart today." You might not feel an instant change, but your heart will begin to settle. Your mind will soften. Your focus will clear. God strengthens you in ways you feel over time, not always all at once.

Your flesh may fail. Your heart may fail. God won't. His strength is steady. His support is constant. He will always be enough.

PART II
Mind Set:
Training Thoughts and Attitudes

Chapter 11

"Whatever you do, work at it with all your heart, as working for the Lord, not for human masters." - Colossians 3:23

There's something special about watching an athlete who gives everything they have, not only in games, but in ordinary moments that no one sees. They run drills with intention. They listen well. They stay focused even when they're tired. They show up early. They stay a few minutes late. Nothing about their effort depends on who's watching. They simply choose to give their best because that's the kind of person they want to be.

This verse from Colossians speaks directly to that mindset. It tells you to work "with all your heart," not halfway, not just enough to get by, and not only when others notice. It gives a reason that changes everything: when you work, you do so for the Lord.

That idea may feel strange at first. After all, you train for your team. You work for your coach. You compete for your school or club. You want to make your family proud.

All those things matter, but this verse reminds you that your deepest motivation should come from your relationship with God. When you give your best because of Him, your purpose becomes bigger than any scoreboard or stat line.

Think about a time when you gave effort only because someone was watching. Maybe you worked harder because your coach stood near your station. Maybe you focused more because you didn't want a teammate to think you were slacking. Those moments don't always feel wrong, but they reveal something: sometimes your motivation rises and falls depending on who is paying attention.

Working with "all your heart" means your effort stays steady regardless of who sees it.

There's freedom in that. When you play or train for the Lord, you don't have to chase people's approval. You don't have to worry about pleasing everyone. You don't have to be controlled by someone else's opinion. You give your best because God deserves your best, and because He sees every moment, even the ones that happen far away from the court, the field, the gym, or the track.

Think about the small moments that build your athletic life: waking up early, stretching when you'd rather rest, practicing skills on your own, fueling your body well, keeping your room organized so you're not rushed, completing homework before practice, or choosing to stay disciplined when distractions show up. These small choices all reveal the condition of your heart.

Working with "all your heart" means being faithful in little things.

Some days, effort flows easily. Your energy feels high. Your confidence feels strong. Your mind feels fresh. On those days, giving your best feels natural.

The verse matters even more on the days when effort feels difficult. Maybe you didn't sleep well. Maybe school drained you. Your emotions could be weighing you down. Maybe you feel frustrated with your progress. On those days, working with all your heart may simply mean showing up. And God honors that too.

This doesn't mean pushing yourself to exhaustion. It means engaging fully with the moment in front of you. Giving what you can, with honesty, with focus, and with a heart that says, "God, I'm doing this for You."

There will be times when your best doesn't look impressive. You might give everything and still fall short. You might try hard and still make mistakes. You might finish last in a sprint or struggle with a drill. That doesn't mean your effort was wasted. God sees the heart behind the action, not just the result. When you offer your effort to Him, He accepts it with joy.

This verse also helps you handle comparison. When you watch other athletes improve faster, jump higher, or move quicker, it's easy to lose heart. It's easy to think, "Why should I try if I'll never catch up?"

Remember: God doesn't measure you against anyone else. He asks only that *you* give *your* best, with the gifts He has given you.

Your best will look different from someone else's best, and that's okay.

Working with all your heart also applies to how you treat people. Your tone toward teammates, your respect for your coach, your patience with younger players, your honesty during tense moments, these are all ways you "work for the Lord." When you respond with humility instead of frustration, when you stay calm instead of snapping, when you choose kindness instead of sarcasm, you are offering something valuable to God.

A heart that works for the Lord doesn't crumble when things go wrong. It doesn't stop trying when the season gets tough. It doesn't quit because a coach makes a comment you don't like. It stays steady because its foundation is obedience.

Jesus showed this kind of heart throughout His life. He served people one by one, even when crowds didn't understand Him. He kept going even when others doubted Him. He did the Father's will in ordinary tasks and in major moments. His example shows you that greatness begins with faithfulness, not applause.

You may feel tempted at times to coast during practice or take shortcuts in drills. Everyone feels that pull, but working with all your heart doesn't mean perfection. It means honesty. It means asking, "Am I giving the effort God deserves?" If the answer feels uncertain, ask Him to shape your attitude. Ask Him to give you endurance. Ask Him to help you stay focused on what matters.

One thing that helps is remembering that effort is a choice you can make even when emotions fluctuate. You may not feel motivated every day, but you can choose to be faithful. You can choose to push through the first few uncomfortable minutes. You can decide to stay engaged. Effort grows stronger with practice.

It also helps to imagine handing your work directly to God. Picture yourself saying, "Lord, I offer this practice to You. I offer this run to You. I offer this drill to You." When you frame your effort that way, tasks feel lighter. You're not working only for a coach's approval. You're working out of love for God.

Before your next practice or training session, take a quiet moment to ask, "What does giving all my heart look like today?" Some days it might look energetic. Other days, it might look steady and simple. Some days it might look like trying again after a mistake. Some days it might look like staying patient when you feel discouraged.

God isn't grading your performance. He is shaping your character.

When you work with all your heart, your sport becomes more than competition. It becomes worship. It becomes a place where you meet God, trust Him, and grow closer to Him.

Give Him your full heart today. He will meet you there with strength, purpose, and joy that lasts far beyond the game.

Chapter 12

"A cheerful heart is good medicine, but a crushed spirit dries up the bones." - Proverbs 17:22

A lot of people think sports are all about physical strength: stronger legs, better stamina, sharper movements, quicker reactions. Those things matter, but ask anyone who has competed for long enough, and they'll tell you something surprising: your heart, not your muscles, often decides how your day goes.

There are times when your body feels fine, but your mood drags everything down. You show up to practice already irritated or discouraged, and suddenly, ordinary drills feel ten times harder. A simple mistake becomes a big deal. You feel slow. You feel heavy. You feel stuck. Nothing "bad" happened, but you can't shake the feeling that something is off.

This verse speaks straight into moments like that. A cheerful heart isn't about pretending everything is perfect. It's about having a spirit that stays open to hope, gratitude, and joy even when life isn't easy. It's about letting God breathe fresh strength into you before negativity takes over.

The writer of Proverbs understood something about human nature: when your heart is lifted, your whole body responds. Things feel lighter. You think more clearly. You face challenges with more confidence.

When your spirit feels crushed, even simple tasks feel impossible.

Young athletes deal with both sides of this more than most people realize.

Think about a practice where everything clicked. Your team laughed between drills. You worked hard, but it didn't feel draining. You walked off the field with a relaxed smile. Maybe nothing huge happened, but your heart felt clear. That's the kind of "medicine" this verse describes: the way joy refreshes you from the inside out.

Now, think of the opposite. A morning when you woke up tired and rushed. A class that frustrated you. A comment someone made that stuck in your head. You tried to shake it off, but it followed you into practice. Suddenly, every mistake felt louder. Every correction felt heavier. You didn't feel like yourself. That's the "crushed spirit" Proverbs describes, when something inside you feels drained, even if your body still has energy.

Here's the good news: God cares deeply about the condition of your heart. He doesn't ignore your emotions. He doesn't expect you to be upbeat every day, but He does want to give you joy that strengthens you from the inside.

A cheerful heart grows from small, steady choices. It often begins with gratitude. Not the forced kind ("I'm thankful because I'm supposed to be"), but the simple habit of noticing what's still good.

You woke up with breath in your lungs. You have teammates who push you and laugh with you. You have coaches who care enough to correct you. You have the chance to train, learn, compete, and grow. These things are easy to miss when you're stressed, but they're gifts.

A cheerful heart also grows when you stop trying to control things you were never meant to carry. You can't control whether your coach gives you more minutes. You can't control how someone else behaves. You can't control the weather, a ref's call, or the bounce of the ball, but you *can* control how you respond. Sometimes, the most freeing choice is to let go of the things that aren't yours to fix.

Joy also shows up when you give yourself space to enjoy your sport again. As athletes grow, the pressure grows. What started as something fun becomes stressful. Expectations rise. Mistakes feel bigger.

Remember: you weren't created just to grind and perform. You were created to live, breathe, enjoy, learn, and grow. When you reconnect with the simple joy of playing, something in your heart wakes up.

Sometimes, joy comes from letting people in. Talking to a teammate. Laughing with a friend. Asking someone to pray for you. Telling a parent or mentor that you feel discouraged. Holding everything inside can crush your spirit one quiet piece at a time. God often uses people to lift you in ways you can't do alone.

There's also a discipline to joy: choosing not to let negativity rule your day. You don't have to deny that something is hard, but you can refuse to let it decide your entire attitude. You can say, "This is tough, but it won't own me." You can remind yourself, "God is here. I can handle this." Those small shifts matter more than they seem.

Think about the athletes you admire. Many of them compete with an ease that looks almost effortless. They're not perfect. They get frustrated too, but they know how to reset their mind, let go of frustration, breathe, and move on. That ability isn't just mental toughness, it's emotional steadiness. It's a cheerful heart anchoring them.

You can grow that too.

Start by noticing your own "warning signs." What crushes your spirit? It could be things like comparison, criticism, pressure from others, or personal expectations that feel impossible. When you notice these patterns, bring them to God instead of pretending they don't exist.

The prayer doesn't have to be long. It can be something simple, like:

"God, my heart feels heavy today. Please lift it."

"Lord, help me find joy again."

"Jesus, steady me."

God hears those simple prayers. He meets you gently. He reminds you that you don't need to force joy, you simply need to make room for Him to restore it.

Another part of a cheerful heart is learning to celebrate small moments. Not just victories, but effort. Growth. Humility. A well-executed drill. A kind conversation. A moment of patience. A recovered mistake. When you celebrate these moments, your heart becomes lighter. You begin to see God at work in places you used to overlook.

As you grow, you'll face days that test your spirit and days that strengthen it. Both matter. Both shape you. Both teach you to rely on God instead of your shifting emotions.

The cheerful heart in this verse is not shallow. It is strong. It is rooted. It is built on trust. When your spirit is lifted by God, not by circumstances, you walk into practice or competition with a steadiness that others notice, sometimes without even knowing why.

Before your next practice, take ten quiet seconds and pray, "Lord, give me a cheerful heart today." That one line can open space for joy, even if the day turns out to be hard.

A cheerful heart won't remove the challenges in front of you, but it will give you strength to face them. And that strength truly is "good medicine", not only for you, but for everyone around you.

Chapter 13

"Train yourself to be godly. For physical training is of some value, but godliness has value for all things, holding promise for both the present life and the life to come." - 1 Timothy 4:7–8

If you've played a sport for even a short amount of time, you know training is part of the deal. Nobody becomes strong by accident. Nobody builds endurance by hoping. Nobody gains skill without repetition. You run drills, lift weights, stretch, study plays, and push yourself in ways most people never see. Training is not always fun, but it shapes you.

Paul, in this letter to Timothy, uses the idea of training to explain something deeper. He points out that physical training matters: it helps your body, sharpens your ability, and prepares you for competition.

He says training yourself to be *godly* matters even more, because that training doesn't fade when the season ends. It stays with you. It shapes who you become, not only as an athlete, but as a person, a leader, a friend, and a follower of Jesus.

Young athletes sometimes think spiritual growth "just happens." They assume they'll become patient if they wait long enough. They assume they'll become humble if life teaches them a lesson or two. They assume they'll trust God more once they hit a certain age.

Paul says it clearly: *train yourself* to be godly. This means growth won't happen by chance. It happens through choice.

Consider the way you train your body. Drills build habits. Repetition builds memory. Conditioning builds toughness. None of it appears overnight. The same is true for your heart. Godliness, things like kindness, self-control, honesty, gratitude, humility, courage, and wisdom, grows the same way muscles grow: through steady, daily practice.

For example, patience develops when you choose not to react the moment frustration shows up. Kindness grows when you encourage a teammate after a mistake. Honesty strengthens when you admit you missed an assignment instead of hiding it. Self-control forms when you breathe instead of snapping back. These moments may feel small, but they add up. They shape you the way simple reps build strength.

Spiritual training often happens in ordinary places: before school, in the locker room, during warm-ups, on the bus, and even at home when you're tired. It happens through the thoughts you choose to hold onto and the ones you choose to release. It happens when you read Scripture for a few quiet minutes and ask God to guide you. It happens when you pray, even briefly, and tell God you want your heart to reflect His character.

Some athletes train with a specific goal in mind. Maybe a faster sprint, a higher jump, or a more accurate shot. In the same way, godly training has goals too. You train to become more like Christ. You train so your reactions look different from the world around you. You train so your confidence comes from God, not from how well or poorly you perform. You train so that you bring peace instead of chaos into a tense moment.

Here's something to notice: both kinds of training require discipline. No athlete wakes up every morning thrilled about conditioning. Some days, you show up because you have to. Some days you're excited. Some days you go through the motions until your heart catches up. Spiritual training works the same way.

There will be days you feel eager to pray, and days you feel distracted. Days when Scripture speaks clearly to your heart, and days when it feels harder to focus.

Remember: Consistency brings results, even when you don't feel them right away.

Many athletes judge their progress too quickly. They assume one bad practice means they're off track. One rough game means they're regressing. One emotional moment means they're failing.

Training doesn't work that way. You don't quit after a single tough day. You show up again tomorrow.

The same is true with godliness. You will have days when you don't react the way you hoped. Days when frustration wins. Days when you feel impatient. Days when you lose focus. A single moment doesn't define your progress. Training is about the long run, not the quick stretch.

Paul also says something encouraging here: physical training has value, but godliness has value for *all* things. That means your spiritual growth reaches places physical training can't touch. It helps you deal with pressure. It shapes your identity. It strengthens you during setbacks. It guides your decisions. It steadies your emotions. It builds wisdom, something you'll need far beyond your athletic years.

Godly training also affects your relationships. A heart shaped by God treats people differently. You listen better. You handle conflict more gently. You apologize sooner. You encourage more often. You celebrate others' success instead of feeling threatened by it. You forgive more quickly. You show compassion instead of judgment. Your heart becomes a place where others feel safe.

Training yourself to be godly also prepares you for moments when life feels uncertain. A strong body can fail you. A sharp mind can get overwhelmed. A fast pace can slow down.

A heart trained to trust God stands firm even when the world around you shifts. You learn to rely on Him instead of relying only on yourself.

Let's bring this back to your daily life as an athlete. Think about a typical week. There are probably practices, games, homework, maybe work, and maybe responsibilities at home. It's easy to let spiritual training slide to the edges. Life feels full, but you don't need long hours to grow. You need intention. Simple, steady steps.

Read Scripture for a few minutes in the morning. Talk to God during your warm-up. Pause for a deep breath when frustration tries to take over. Tell God what's on your mind as you walk to your next class. Ask Him to guide your attitude before practice. Thank Him for something good at the end of the day.

Small steps. Daily reps. Quiet growth.

Over time, these choices build a strong heart: a heart able to handle adversity with calmness, a heart quick to love others, a heart patient with itself, a heart that reflects Jesus.

Before your next practice or workout, take a moment and pray, "Lord, train my heart today." Let that be your starting point.

Because training your body shapes the athlete you are today, but training your heart shapes the person you'll be for the rest of your life.

Chapter 14

"Peace I leave with you; my peace I give you. I do not give to you as the world gives. Do not let your hearts be troubled and do not be afraid." - John 14:27

Pressure shows up in so many ways for young athletes. Sometimes it comes from a coach expecting more from you. Sometimes it comes from teammates watching how you respond in tough moments. Sometimes it comes from parents hoping to see you shine. And sometimes the pressure doesn't come from anyone else at all: it comes from inside you.

You hold yourself to a certain standard.

You want to perform well.

You want to avoid letting people down.

You want to feel proud of what you bring to the game.

When something doesn't go the way you hoped, peace is usually the first thing to disappear. Your chest tightens. Your mind speeds up. You replay mistakes again and again. You wonder what others are thinking. You wonder what this means for your future. It's amazing how fast one moment can scatter your thoughts.

Jesus speaks straight into that feeling in John 14:27, offering something far deeper than ordinary calm. *"Peace I leave with you; my peace I give you."*

Not the temporary kind of peace the world offers: the kind that collapses as soon as something goes wrong.

Not peace based on perfect performances.

Not peace based on being praised.

Not peace based on everything going your way.

He gives **His** peace.

The same peace that steadied Him through storms, crowds, critics, exhaustion, betrayal, and the cross itself.

A peace that does not shatter.

A peace that does not fade when life gets loud.

A peace that holds steady even when your world feels shaken.

Most young athletes think peace comes after everything settles. Jesus says peace comes **before** that, because it comes from Him.

He places it into your hands.

He places it into your heart.

He places it into the very places where anxiety tries to live.

When Jesus says, *"Do not let your hearts be troubled,"* He isn't ignoring your stress. He knows you face pressure. He knows fear whispers at the worst times. He knows how easy it is to look confident on the outside while your mind is spinning inside. He isn't telling you to force calmness or pretend nothing is wrong. He's inviting you to let Him steady the places that shake.

"Do not be afraid" doesn't mean fear disappears forever. It means fear doesn't get to lead you.

Think about moments when your peace slips away.

Maybe a mistake early in a game throws you off.

Maybe you're afraid of disappointing a coach.

Maybe you feel overlooked.

Maybe you feel misunderstood.

Maybe you want to prove yourself so badly that every misstep feels crushing.

In those moments, peace feels distant because the world trains you to hold everything tightly: your performance, your identity, your reputation, your progress. Because you're holding all of that by yourself, even little things feel heavy.

Jesus offers something different. Not a bigger load, but a lighter heart.

His peace doesn't come from trying harder. It comes from trusting deeper.

Picture your heart like a room with lights and windows. When anxiety grows, the room darkens. When pressure builds, the walls feel closer. When fear gets loud, the whole space tightens.

When Jesus steps into that room with His peace, something shifts. He doesn't force the pressure out. He fills the room with His presence until the pressure no longer has power.

His peace doesn't remove challenges. It changes how you move through them.

You've probably noticed how some athletes stay calm during intense moments. They don't panic when they fall behind. They don't lose their composure when they make a mistake. They compete with a steady confidence that isn't tied to the scoreboard.

That steadiness often comes from something deeper than skill. It comes from knowing who they are and where their strength rests.

Jesus offers you that same steadiness.

He doesn't promise that every game will go your way. He doesn't promise that you'll never feel nervous again. He promises that His peace can sit in your heart even when nerves rise. He promises that you don't have to face pressure alone. He promises that fear cannot rule you if He lives within you.

"My peace I give you."

Let those words rest for a moment.

His peace.

Given freely.

Given personally.

Given to you.

There's a difference between calmness and Christ's peace. Calmness fades. Christ's peace remains. Calmness depends on circumstances. Christ's peace depends on His presence. Calmness can feel fragile.

Christ's peace is strong enough to carry you.

As an athlete, you will face tension, conflict, tough losses, unexpected changes, and moments when confidence slides. Jesus doesn't ask you to pretend you're okay. He invites you to bring every anxious corner of your heart to Him.

Take a moment to think about what steals your peace most often.

A certain pressure?

A certain teammate?

A certain fear?

A certain expectation you've placed on yourself?

Now, imagine handing that weight to Jesus. Not in a dramatic way, just in a quiet, honest moment. Imagine Him placing His peace where that pressure once sat.

Peace doesn't have to be loud to be real.

Sometimes peace feels like a deep breath that reaches places you didn't know were tight.

Sometimes it feels like a soft voice inside saying, "You're okay. Keep going. I'm with you."

Sometimes it feels like the slow unclenching of your chest after a tough moment.

Sometimes it feels like a steady confidence rising quietly inside you.

Jesus gives peace that stays.

Before your next practice or competition, step aside for just a few seconds.

Close your eyes, breathe slowly, and whisper, "Jesus, give me Your peace." You don't need fancy words. You don't need a long prayer. You just need honesty.

You may feel something shift immediately. Or you may simply walk into the moment with a sense of being held. Either way, His peace is there. You are not carrying this alone.

The world will always offer pressure.

Jesus will always offer peace.

Choose the One who steadies your heart.

Let His peace fill the places where fear once lived.

Let His peace anchor you when things feel uncertain.

Let His peace remind you that you are supported, loved, and never alone.

Because the One who gives peace is the One who walks every step with you.

Chapter 15

"He says, "Be still, and know that I am God; I will be exalted among the nations, I will be exalted in the earth." - Psalm 46:10

Stillness feels almost impossible in the life of a young athlete. There's always someplace to be, something to improve, something to prepare for, something coming next. You move from school to practice to homework to family responsibilities. Even on your days off, your mind keeps racing, thinking about the next game, the next skill, the next chance to prove yourself.

Because of that, this short verse from Psalm 46 often feels out of place. *Be still?* In the middle of everything? In the middle of pressure, expectations, noise, and stress? How does stillness even fit into a life that demands so much movement?

This verse carries a quiet strength. It doesn't say "be still" because nothing is happening. It says "be still" because something is happening, and you need space to notice it. God is working. God is present. God is leading, but when your life becomes too loud, you stop hearing Him.

Most athletes know what it feels like to prepare for a big moment. Before a race starts, before a serve, before a free throw, before stepping onto the mat, field, or court, there's a pause. A breath. A brief silence before action. That tiny pause is often where focus is gathered. It's where everything shifts from scattered thoughts to clear intention.

This verse invites you into a deeper kind of pause. Not only before a game. Not only during a timeout, but in your life.

"Be still" is not about doing nothing. It's about creating space for God to remind you who He is.

Many young athletes carry pressure without realizing how heavy it is. Pressure to perform. Pressure to improve. Pressure to please coaches and parents. Pressure to be steady at school. Pressure to hold everything together even on days when you feel far from steady. All that weight builds up quietly until you reach a point where your heart feels stretched thin.

Stillness is God's gift in those moments. It's His invitation to set the weight down, even just for a few minutes.

Picture yourself after a busy day. You've rushed from class to practice, you've given all you had, and your mind won't stop spinning. In that moment, God whispers the same truth He whispered thousands of years ago: *Be still. I am God. You are not carrying this alone.*

Stillness can feel uncomfortable at first. When you sit quietly, thoughts you've ignored finally surface. Worries, fears, memories, questions, things you've pushed aside show up. Many athletes avoid stillness for that very reason. It feels easier to stay busy than to face what's happening inside.

When God calls you to be still, He isn't trying to overwhelm you. He's trying to heal you. He's trying to free your heart from the noise that exhausts you. He's trying to remind you that your life is held by Someone stronger than the pressure you feel.

Stillness helps you remember three things:

1. You don't have to be in control of everything.

You work hard. You train. You prepare, but you cannot control outcomes. You cannot control other people's choices. You cannot control the future. Stillness teaches you to release what is not yours to hold.

2. God is with you, even when you don't feel Him.

Life moves fast, and in the rush, God can feel far away, but stillness opens your eyes to His presence again. You remember that He has been walking with you the entire time.

3. Your identity is not built on performance.

When you pause long enough to meet God, the pressure around you loses its grip. You start to see yourself the way God sees you, loved, chosen, steady, and valuable apart from what you accomplish.

Consider how athletes use rest. After a workout, the body needs recovery. Muscles rebuild. Strength returns. Without rest, you break down. Without rest, you burn out. In the same way, your heart needs spiritual rest. Stillness allows God to restore what stress has worn down.

Sometimes, stillness looks like closing your eyes for thirty seconds before practice and taking one slow breath. Sometimes it looks like lying in bed at night with a quiet prayer. Sometimes it's sitting alone for a few minutes before school, letting the day settle in your mind. Sometimes, it's opening Scripture and letting one verse steady your thoughts.

Stillness isn't about getting everything right. It's about showing up with honesty.

You might say, "God, today I feel worried."

Or, "Lord, I don't know what to do."

Or, "I feel off and I can't explain why."

Or even, "I'm tired, please help me."

Every one of those prayers is an act of stillness. Every one of them brings you closer to the truth: God is God, and you are not asked to handle life alone.

When you learn how to be still, you also learn how to compete with more peace. Instead of panicking after mistakes, you breathe. Instead of worrying about what others think, you anchor yourself in God's voice. Instead of rushing through every moment, you become more aware of what's actually happening. You play with clarity instead of cluttered thoughts.

Stillness does not make you passive. It makes you stronger. It centers you. It grounds you. It helps you make better decisions because your heart is no longer clouded by noise.

There's another piece of this verse worth noticing: "Know that I am God."

This is the heart of everything.

Stillness is awareness. Awareness of God's power. Awareness of His love. Awareness of His control. Awareness of His goodness when your circumstances don't look good. Awareness that He sees the parts of you that others miss. Awareness that He knows the path ahead, even when you feel lost.

Your stillness becomes a place where trust grows.

Maybe you've been carrying stress quietly. Maybe your season hasn't gone how you hoped. Maybe you're battling doubt or fear of failure. Possibly, you're stretching yourself so thin that you can't even remember the last time you felt calm. God meets you here and says, *Be still. Let Me hold you. Let Me be your God.*

Before your next practice or game, find a moment, even ten seconds, and pause.

Take one deep breath.

Whisper, "Lord, help me be still."

Let that be enough.

Over time, these small moments will shape you into an athlete who moves with peace instead of panic, clarity instead of chaos, trust instead of fear.

Stillness isn't the absence of effort. It's the presence of God.

That presence will carry you through everything ahead.

Chapter 16

"Instead, speaking the truth in love, we will grow to become in every respect the mature body of him who is the head, that is, Christ." - Ephesians 4:15

Sports bring out strong emotions. You feel excitement, pressure, disappointment, pride, frustration, and joy, sometimes all in the same afternoon. With so much going on inside you, your words can rise quickly. A comment slips out without much thought. A reaction comes before your mind catches up. A teammate's mistake sparks something in you that you didn't mean to say aloud.

Words move fast in competitive environments. Once they're spoken, you can't take them back.

That's what makes this verse is so important. God calls you to "speak the truth in love." Notice both parts of that instruction. Truth matters. Love matters. Neither stands alone. Truth without love can sound harsh or cold.

Love without truth can become shallow or avoidant, but when truth and love work together, they create something strong, steady, and mature.

A young athlete lives in a world where honesty is often loud but not gentle, and kindness is sometimes gentle but not honest. This verse gives you a different path, one that builds people instead of tearing them down.

Think about a team you've been part of. At some point, someone probably spoke the truth to you. Maybe a coach told you what needed improvement. Maybe a teammate corrected your positioning. Maybe a friend pointed out a habit that was hurting your game. Truth is not always comfortable, but it helps you grow. How that truth is delivered makes all the difference.

You've probably heard truth spoken in a way that felt sharp. Has someone's tone embarrassed you? Maybe the timing was off, or the words were right, but the attitude behind them made you shut down. On the flip side, maybe you've heard words that were loving but never honest, encouragement that felt nice but didn't help you improve.

Paul says real maturity requires both.

Speaking the truth in love means you care about people enough to be honest, but humble enough to speak gently.

For young athletes, this plays out in many ways.

Think about how you handle frustration in a game. When a teammate misses an assignment or makes a mistake, what rises in you? Do you snap? Do you criticize? Do you stay silent but stew with irritation? Or do you find a way to communicate that helps instead of harms?

Speaking the truth in love sounds like, "Hey, it's all right, next time try cutting sooner." It sounds like, "You've got this. Let's reset." It sounds like support wrapped around guidance.

It never sounds like shame.

What about yourself? Some athletes speak harshly to others, but many speak even harsher words to themselves. You may feel tempted to mutter, "I'm terrible," or "I can't get anything right," or "I always mess up." Those statements may feel true in the moment, but they're not spoken in love, and God never instructs you to tear yourself down.

Speaking truth in love to yourself might sound like, "That wasn't my best, but I can learn from it," or "This is hard, but I'm growing," or "I made a mistake, but it doesn't define me." Honest. Loving. Balanced.

This verse also challenges you in relationships. Maybe you have a teammate who brings negative energy into the group. Maybe a friend keeps saying things that hurt others. Maybe someone is drifting away from discipline, effort, or good choices.

Speaking truth in love doesn't mean ignoring issues because you want to stay comfortable. It means approaching the person with respect and care, not to prove a point or gain power, but to help them grow.

A loving truth might be, "I care about you, and I've noticed you seem frustrated lately. Want to talk about it?"

Or, "I see you getting down on yourself. You're more capable than you think, how can I support you?"

Or even, "I respect you, and I need to be honest: that comment in practice today felt hurtful. Can we talk about it?"

Truth spoken in love helps teams strengthen instead of fracture.

This verse also asks something of you when you are the one receiving truth. Sometimes, the hardest part is hearing feedback without taking it as an attack. Growing athletes learn to welcome correction. Not because it feels good, but because it shapes them into better teammates and better people.

When someone speaks truth in love to you, take a moment before reacting. Ask yourself, "Is there something here that can help me grow?" If there is, thank the person, even if it stings a little. If the delivery wasn't perfect, be gracious. Remember, everyone is learning how to speak truth in love, not just you.

Love can also guide you to stay silent at the right times. Not every thought needs to be spoken. Not every frustration needs to be voiced. Not every truth needs to be shared immediately. Wisdom knows when to speak and when to wait. Sometimes speaking the truth in love means giving someone space to cool off before addressing an issue. Sometimes it means praying about your words before you say them.

Jesus modeled this kind of speech perfectly. He spoke truths that challenged people, yet He did it with compassion. He corrected His followers, yet His tone invited them rather than pushed them away. His words carried clarity, not cruelty. When He spoke truth, people felt convicted but also loved.

You will never speak perfectly like Jesus, but you can follow His example.

Before addressing a teammate or friend, ask yourself:

Is what I'm about to say true?

Is it loving?

Is it necessary?

Is it helpful?

Those simple questions can save you from unnecessary conflict and help you build deeper trust with the people around you.

There's another layer to this verse: the more you speak truth in love, the more you grow. Words shape relationships, but they also shape you. When you choose honesty wrapped in kindness, you develop patience. You develop gentleness. You develop courage. You become someone others trust, a person who doesn't hide from truth but doesn't weaponize it either.

As you train your body, train your speech. Let your words become part of your character training. Speak truthfully, but let love color the tone.

Before your next practice, whisper a simple prayer:

"Lord, help my words bring life today."

Not pressure. Not fear. Not sarcasm. Life.

Because when you speak truth in love, you reflect Christ in what you do and how you communicate. That kind of maturity reaches far beyond your sport.

Chapter 17

"Do to others as you would have them do to you." - Luke 6:31

Every athlete knows what it feels like to be treated poorly: an eye roll after a mistake, a sarcastic comment at the wrong moment, a teammate who blames you for something you didn't cause, or a coach who seems frustrated before you've even started. Those moments stay with you. You feel them in your chest. They can change how you play, how you think, and how you see yourself.

Jesus knew that everyone wants to be treated with respect and kindness. That's why He said to treat others the way you want to be treated. It's a simple idea, but it matters. It shapes teams, friendships, the places where you compete, and even who you become.

For a young athlete, this verse isn't something to hang only on a classroom wall. It belongs on the court, the field, the track, the pool deck, the weight room, the locker room, everywhere competition and emotion collide.

Think about how you want others to treat you when you're having an off day. You want patience, not judgment. You want someone to believe in you even when you don't believe in yourself. You want grace for your mistakes. You want honesty delivered with care. You want encouragement in moments when you feel small.

Now flip that around: Jesus calls you to offer those things first.

Treat others the way you *wish* they treated you, not the way they *actually* treat you.

This is where the challenge begins. It's easy to be kind to people who are kind back. It's easy to support teammates who always support you. It's easy to respect someone who respects you.

Jesus didn't say, "Treat others the way they treat you." He raised the standard higher. He went straight to your heart.

This verse becomes real in moments when kindness feels unnatural, when you're tired, annoyed, embarrassed, or frustrated.

Imagine a teammate who makes the same mistake again. You have a choice: respond with irritation or respond with the same grace you'd want if the roles were reversed.

Imagine a coach correcting you in a tone you don't like. You have a choice: respond with disrespect in your attitude, or respond with the level of respect you hope someone would show you if you were the coach.

Imagine someone leaves you out of something. You have a choice: shut them out in return or offer the same inclusion you wish you'd received.

This way of living doesn't come from instinct. It comes from intention. It comes from choosing to honor Christ more than your emotions in the moment.

Every team has someone who sets the tone. Sometimes, it's the captain. Sometimes, it's the quiet kid who never snaps. Sometimes it's the athlete who stays steady under pressure. You don't need a title to set the tone; you just need a heart shaped by Jesus' words.

Treating others well can transform a team faster than talent ever could.

Picture a practice where everyone encourages the next person in line. Picture a locker room where people speak up for each other, not against each other. Picture a huddle where honesty and love work together. Picture a bench that celebrates every effort. Picture teammates lifting each other instead of competing for attention.

This is the kind of atmosphere Jesus encouraged, a place where people see each other clearly, value each other, and act with compassion.

Treating others well doesn't always come easily. Some personalities rub you the wrong way. Some people test your patience. Some relationships feel complicated. Besides, the pressure of sports can make even small interactions feel sharp.

This is why you need Jesus' help. You don't treat others well because you're naturally perfect. You treat others well because Jesus treated *you* with kindness first. When you look at the way He interacted with people, the patient, gentle, wise, steady way He handled difficult moments, you begin to understand how He wants you to treat the people around you.

He doesn't ask you to do it alone.

When you feel your patience slipping, ask Him for calmness.

When you feel jealousy creeping in, ask Him for gratitude.

When you feel annoyed, ask Him for gentleness.

When you feel tempted to say something sharp, ask Him for restraint.

When you feel hurt, ask Him for strength not to hurt others back.

A quiet prayer in the middle of conflict can change your whole reaction. Even a simple breath can give you enough space to choose love instead of frustration.

Treating others well doesn't mean avoiding truth. If a teammate needs correction, you can give it. If someone is hurting you, you can speak up. If conflict needs addressing, you can address it.

The *way* you speak matters. Jesus' instruction anchors your attitude in dignity and compassion.

There's something else to notice: this verse helps you love yourself too. When you start treating others with more grace, you eventually turn some of that grace inward. You become slower to tear yourself down. You begin to understand that God wants you to show the same kindness to yourself that you offer to others.

This verse helps to build maturity, the kind that comes with wisdom. It teaches you that strength isn't only physical. Strength includes emotional control, humility, patience, and the ability to rise above pettiness. It teaches you that leadership isn't loud. Leadership is consistent. It's the person who does what's right even when it's unnoticed.

As you move forward in your season, look for small moments where you can live this out:

Hold the door.

Welcome someone new.

Encourage a teammate who's struggling.

Apologize quickly.

Step back when your reaction feels too strong.

Share equipment.

Offer grace.

It doesn't have to be dramatic. It just has to be sincere.

Before your next practice or game, take a moment and pray, "Lord, help me treat others the way I hope to be treated today." You'd be surprised how often that simple prayer changes the way you see people.

Jesus gave this verse knowing how powerful it is. When you live it out, you show His love, on and off the field. You honor Him with your character. And you become the kind of athlete others feel safe around, encouraged by, and strengthened through.

Do to others what you wish they would do for you. In that simple command, entire seasons can change. And so can you.

Chapter 18

"Therefore, as God's chosen people, holy and dearly loved, clothe yourselves with compassion, kindness, humility, gentleness and patience."
- Colossians 3:12

Most athletes think about what they wear every day. Uniforms, warm-ups, gear, school clothes, each one signals something: What team you play for, what sport you love, and whether you're ready to compete. Clothing sends messages long before you open your mouth.

In this verse, Paul uses the image of clothing to describe something far more important than fabric. He tells believers to clothe themselves with kindness, compassion, humility, gentleness, and patience. He says not just feel those things, not just think about them. Wear them, wrap them around yourself the same way you pull on a jersey before stepping onto the field.

Kindness is not something you wait to feel. It's something you put on.

Paul begins by reminding you who you are: chosen, holy, dearly loved by God. Before you choose kindness, you remember your identity. You don't act kindly because you're trying to impress others. You show kindness because God loves you, claims you, and forms you into someone who reflects Him.

Young athletes sometimes underestimate kindness. Not because they're unkind people, but because sports can be intense. Competition tightens your focus. You think about your assignment, your timing, your role, your strategy. In the middle of all that, kindness feels like a soft skill, nice to have, but not essential.

Remember: kindness is essential. It changes teams. It builds trust. It settles conflict. It opens communication. It keeps frustration from spreading like wildfire. Kindness has the power to turn a tense practice into a productive one, a struggling teammate into a confident one, and a fractured group into something unified.

Kindness is visible. People feel it the moment you walk into a room or step onto a field.

Paul describes kindness as clothing because it isn't meant to be hidden. When you clothe yourself with something, others see it. The same is true with kindness. Your teammates see it, your coaches feel it, your classmates notice it, and even opponents experience it.

Consider the opposite for a moment. You've probably been around athletes who wear frustration like a jacket. Even before they speak, you can sense it: closed shoulders, quick reactions, sharp tone, rolling eyes. You don't even need to ask if something's wrong; the attitude announces itself. That kind of presence weighs down the group.

Kindness works in the same way, but it lifts instead of weighs down. A kind presence brings calmness. It gives people space to breathe. It makes mistakes feel safe to correct. It builds the kind of environment where growth happens.

What does kindness look like in real moments?

It looks like giving a teammate grace when they're struggling, not judgment.

It looks like offering a seat next to you when someone seems left out.

It looks like smiling at the freshman who feels out of place.

It looks like high-fiving the teammate who rarely gets attention.

It looks like helping someone gather equipment without being asked.

It looks like speaking calmly when the game gets heated.

It looks like apologizing when you know you hurt someone, even if it feels awkward.

Kindness is rarely loud. It's steady, simple, and surprisingly powerful.

Kindness is not always easy. Some days, you feel stretched thin. Some days, your patience ends before practice even starts. Some days, someone says something careless, and you feel the urge to snap. Some days, you don't feel like dressing yourself with anything except quiet frustration.

Those are the days this verse matters most.

When you "clothe" yourself with kindness, you choose it *before* the day tests you. Just like you don't wait until midday to put on your shoes, you don't wait until you're irritated to decide whether to be kind. You decide in advance.

"Lord, help me put on kindness today." That one sentence changes your posture.

Here's the part many people overlook: kindness is not weakness, but strength under control. Anyone can react sharply when they're annoyed, or match someone else's bad attitude. Anyone can roll their eyes and mutter something under their breath.

That's easy, but kindness requires discipline. Kindness takes maturity. Kindness takes courage, especially when the atmosphere around you feels tense or negative.

Jesus lived this out beautifully. He didn't treat people based on their mood or performance. He responded to their hearts, not their mistakes. He stopped for people others ignored. He spoke gently when others shouted. He welcomed those who felt unworthy. Kindness ran through everything He did.

When you choose kindness, you look like Him.

You may not always see the results immediately. You might offer kindness to someone who doesn't respond well. You might speak gently and still feel ignored. You might encourage someone and never hear a "thank you."

Your kindness is not wasted. It plants seeds in people's hearts. It builds a reputation for trust. It honors God even when no one praises you for it.

It also protects your own spirit. When you choose kindness, you guard your heart from bitterness. You push back against negativity trying to settle inside you. You remind yourself that you are not controlled by the behavior of others, you are guided by Christ.

Kindness also makes you a better competitor. An athlete who is calm, patient, and centered performs better than one who is angry or distracted. Kindness steadies your emotions. It keeps your head clear. It keeps your reactions disciplined. It helps you handle pressure with peace instead of panic.

Think about a game where everyone lost their cool. Chaos spreads quickly, snapping, blaming, arguing.

Think about a team grounded in kindness. They communicate better. They adjust faster. They move past mistakes without melting down. That advantage cannot be measured in stats, but it's real.

As you step into each day, remember the order of the verse: you clothe yourself with kindness *because* God calls you His own. Your kindness flows out of the love He has already given you.

Before your next practice or school day, try this simple prayer: "Lord, help me wear kindness today. Help me treat others the way You've treated me."

Let that prayer shape your tone.

Let it shape your reactions.

Let it shape your posture.

When you put on kindness, you're preparing to reflect Christ in every moment.

Chapter 19

"A gentle answer turns away wrath, but a harsh word stirs up anger." - *Proverbs 15:1*

If you've played sports for any length of time, you know how quickly emotions can swing. A close call, a teammate's mistake, a coach's tone, or a moment of pressure can turn calm athletes into frustrated ones. You might feel your jaw tighten, your breath shorten, or a sharp comment rise in your throat before you even realize it. Moments like that happen fast. What you choose to say next matters.

Proverbs 15:1 gives a simple but powerful reminder: your response can either calm a situation or ignite it. Not your talent. Not your position. Not your speed. Your *words*.

Athletes often underestimate how much influence they carry with their voice. You don't need to be a team captain to shift the temperature of a room. You don't need to be the best player to change the tone of a conversation. A single sentence can cool down tension or turn it into something much worse.

A soft answer doesn't mean a weak one. It means a measured one. A wise one. A controlled one. It means you choose calmness over reaction. You choose thoughtfulness over impulse. You choose peace over winning the argument.

Think back to a moment when someone snapped at you, like a teammate who was irritated after a mistake. Maybe it was a coach who raised their voice. Perhaps it was an opponent who said something they shouldn't have. How did your heart respond? Even if you stayed quiet on the outside, something inside you likely flared up.

Now imagine a moment when someone responded to your frustration with gentleness. When you expected anger, but got patience instead. When you braced for conflict, but heard calmness. Those moments stay with you, too, but in a better way. They show you what's possible when someone chooses self-control.

A soft answer is not about pretending everything is fine. It's about refusing to add fuel to a fire.

In sports, fire grows fast.

One harsh comment in a huddle can split a team.

One angry outburst on the sideline can distract everyone.

One sarcastic remark can tear down trust.

One shouted accusation can turn teammates into opponents.

You've seen it happen. You might have been right in the middle of it. Maybe you've felt the sting of someone's reckless words, or later regretted your own.

You are in an environment where emotions run high and mistakes are visible. You can't hide. People see your reactions. They hear them. They remember them.

A soft answer doesn't mean you ignore problems. You can correct someone. You can ask questions. You can express frustration, but the *way* you do it sets the tone.

A calm "Hey, let's fix this together" breaks tension.

A sharp "What are you doing?" multiplies it.

A steady "Next time, shift sooner" encourages growth.

A loud "You always mess that up" crushes someone's spirit.

A simple "I hear you, let's talk about it" opens the door to peace.

A mocking "Relax, you're overreacting" slams it shut.

Your words have weight, more than you think.

Sometimes, the hardest person to give a soft answer to is yourself. Athletes often speak to themselves in ways they'd never speak to a friend. After a mistake, you might hear yourself mutter insults under your breath.

After a tough day, you might replay every error, adding cruel comments each time. Your spirit feels the impact of your own voice.

A soft answer toward yourself sounds like, "That wasn't my best, but I'm learning," or "I can reset and try again," or "This moment doesn't define me." Kindness counts inward too.

Soft answers are difficult. When you feel attacked, your first instinct is to defend. When you feel embarrassed, your instinct is to snap. When you feel unheard, your instinct is to raise your volume. Your reactions rise out of instinct, not intention.

That's where God steps in.

You won't naturally choose soft answers every time. You need the Holy Spirit to guide your tongue. You need God to catch you in that split second between impulse and speech. You need Him to calm your racing heart, steady your breathing, and remind you that peace is always an option, even when frustration is screaming for your attention.

Before responding in a heated moment, even one slow breath can change everything. Breath creates space. Space creates perspective. Perspective gives you room to choose gentleness. It sounds simple, but it takes practice.

A soft answer also requires humility. You have to admit that you don't gain anything by winning a shouting match. You don't become stronger by belittling someone. You don't become a better athlete by tearing down teammates. Humility lets you see the bigger picture: you are part of something larger than your pride.

It's also helpful to remember this: most anger comes from fear. Fear of letting people down, fear of being misunderstood, fear of losing control, fear of not being good enough. When someone reacts harshly toward you, there's often more happening under the surface. A soft answer speaks to their deeper fear rather than their loud expression.

You might be surprised how often someone softens when they're met with gentleness. Anger feels strong, but it's fragile. A gentle response can disarm it completely.

There will be times when a soft answer won't fix the situation instantly. Some people stay angry. Some refuse to listen. Some project their emotions onto you no matter how calm you remain. Your responsibility is not controlling their reaction, it's honoring God with yours.

Over time, your consistent gentleness builds your reputation. People trust those who remain steady in conflict. They listen better. They seek advice. They feel safe around you, and you become someone who carries peace into tense environments.

Before your next practice or game, pray a simple prayer:

"Lord, guide my words today. Help me bring calm, not chaos."

Say it again when a teammate snaps.

Say it again when you feel frustration building in your chest.

Say it again when your own thoughts start turning sharp.

Let God shape your speech the same way He shapes your heart.

A soft answer is not weakness. It is strength expressed with maturity. It's choosing wisdom when emotion tries to lead. It's honoring God in the middle of conflict.

It's one of the marks of a truly strong athlete: someone who carries peace, not pressure, into every room.

Chapter 20

"In the same way, let your light shine before others, that they may see your good deeds and glorify your Father in heaven." - Matthew 5:16

Every athlete brings something into the room the moment they walk in. Some bring energy. Some bring quiet confidence. Some bring calmness. Some bring tension. Some bring joy. You can feel it before a drill even starts. The way someone carries themselves changes the atmosphere around them.

Jesus knew this about people long before sports teams existed. That's why He used the image of light. Light doesn't try to get attention. It doesn't force people to notice it. It simply shines, and because it shines, darkness loses its power. People can see. People can move. People feel safer. Light changes everything, just by being what it is.

In this verse, Jesus tells you that you are meant to shine. Not in an arrogant, "look at me" way, but in a way that reflects God's goodness. Your life, your attitude, your choices, your character, your effort, and your kindness are all ways you shine.

Young athletes sometimes worry about standing out too much. They don't want to seem prideful. They don't want to draw attention. They don't want people judging them.

The kind of shining Jesus talks about has nothing to do with bragging or showing off. It has everything to do with letting God's work in you become visible through the way you treat people.

Think about a teammate who always lifts others up. Someone who encourages during tough drills, who laughs easily, who works hard without complaining, who doesn't talk badly about anyone. When that teammate walks into the gym or onto the field, things feel different. They shine without trying to.

That's the kind of light Jesus calls you to shine.

Your light might look like patience during a rough practice.

It might look like honesty when no one else is being honest.

It might look like staying positive when your team falls behind.

It might look like helping someone who feels out of place.

It might look like treating opponents with respect.

It might look like apologizing first, even when you don't want to.

It might look like giving your full effort on a day when you're tired or discouraged.

Light shows up in ordinary ways.

Jesus didn't say you *might* shine. He said you *are* the light. The challenge is not to create light but to stop covering it. Many things can dim your light: fear, insecurity, comparison, anger, jealousy, frustration, or embarrassment. When these things take over, your light doesn't shine as brightly.

Some athletes dim their light because they're afraid of what others might think. They hold back kindness. They avoid standing up for someone. They don't speak encouragement out loud even when they feel it. They worry they'll look strange or too serious about their faith.

Jesus calls you to shine anyway.

Not because you're perfect.

Not because you have it all figured out, but because the world around you needs light, more than you realize.

Think about the people in your circle. Some are carrying quiet struggles you never hear about. Some feel unseen. Some doubt themselves every day. Some don't know how to ask for help. Some are overwhelmed by expectations. When you shine with kindness and grace, you give them something to hold onto.

Your light points them toward hope.

The beautiful thing about light is that it doesn't have to be bright to matter. Even a small light can guide someone through darkness. A single kind word can change someone's day. A simple act of patience can calm a tense moment. A gentle tone can soften someone's anger.

Jesus says your light helps others "see your good deeds and glorify your Father in heaven." That means your light isn't meant to draw praise to yourself. It's meant to point people toward God. When people see something different in you, peace under pressure, patience in frustration, kindness when others are harsh, they begin to wonder what's behind it. They begin to see God's character through your conduct.

You may think your influence is small, but you never know who is watching. You never know whose heart is softened by your consistency. You never know whose confidence grows because you believed in them. You never know which younger teammate looks up to you. You never know which coach sees your work ethic and is encouraged by it.

Shining your light doesn't mean pretending you're fine all the time. It doesn't mean hiding your struggles. It doesn't mean acting perfect. In fact, some of your brightest moments may come when you handle your own weakness with humility and honesty. People notice when someone stays gentle after messing up. They notice when someone refuses to blame others. They notice when someone owns their mistakes. That kind of humility shines.

Light is strongest in darkness. When things get difficult, when the team is frustrated, when the season feels long, when a game doesn't go well, your light matters even more. Anyone can shine when everything is easy. Real maturity shines when circumstances are tough.

Your light might feel small, but small lights add up. If even a few athletes choose to shine, the atmosphere of a team can change. Negativity loses its grip. Encouragement spreads. Trust grows. Conversations become healthier. People treat each other better.

The question is not whether you have light. You do. The question is whether you'll choose to shine it.

Before your next practice or game, take a few seconds to breathe and pray, "Lord, help me shine Your light today." That simple prayer sets your heart in the right place.

As the day unfolds, look for moments where your light can bring peace:

A teammate struggling? Shine.

A coach stressed? Shine.

A game slipping away? Shine.

A mistake embarrassing you? Shine.

A friend hurting quietly? Shine.

Light isn't something you force. It's something you choose.

Live with dignity.

Speak with kindness.

Compete with integrity.

Apologize with humility.

Encourage with boldness.

Honor God quietly and consistently.

That is how your light shines.

Let your life glow with God's goodness, one small moment at a time. The world sees more than you think. God uses every bit of light you offer.

PART III
Body Set:
Competing With Discipline

Chapter 21

"Do everything without grumbling or arguing, so that you may become **blameless** *and* *pure,* *"children of God without fault in a warped and crooked generation. Then you will shine among them like stars in the sky"* *- Philippians 2:14-15*

Every athlete knows what it feels like to be asked to do something you don't really want to do. Maybe it's an extra conditioning run, a drill you dread, a correction you didn't expect, or a tough practice on a day when you're already tired. Your body reacts first. You sigh a little, or your shoulders slump, or you mumble under your breath. Sometimes, it's quiet. Sometimes, it's loud, but you feel the grumbling rise inside you.

Paul's words in Philippians may sound simple, but they press into something that affects teams more than most people realize: attitude. Not talent. Not speed. Not game IQ. Attitude. The way you respond when things get tough or inconvenient says a lot about the condition of your heart.

"Do all things without grumbling or arguing." It feels impossible at first. Who goes through life without complaining?

Paul isn't asking for a fake smile. He's pointing toward a deeper kind of maturity, a maturity that shows up not in comfort, but in challenge.

Grumbling is quiet resistance. Arguing is loud resistance. Both drain your joy and the joy of everyone around you.

Think about a day when the mood of your whole team seemed off. Maybe one person complained about the warmup. Then someone else rolled their eyes during a drill. Then someone muttered something about the coach. Before long, the whole practice felt heavy. The work wasn't harder than usual, but the atmosphere was different. Complaints spread like a small spark catching dry grass.

Now, picture the opposite. Picture a day when practice was tough, but someone stayed positive. Someone said, "Let's go," with real energy. Someone embraced the challenge instead of shrinking from it. Someone encouraged others during conditioning. That person carried a spark, too, one that lifted the team instead of dragging it down.

This is what Paul meant when he said you can "shine like stars." Stars don't try to shine; they just shine, and the darkness around them makes their light even more visible. Your attitude has that same effect. When others complain, and you choose gratitude, you shine.

When others argue, and you choose peace, you shine. When others give half effort, and you choose full effort, you shine.

God uses your steady spirit to point people toward Him.

For a young athlete, the temptation to grumble comes from many places. Sometimes, it's tiredness, frustration, or disappointment.

Sometimes, the feeling that things aren't fair. Sometimes, a coach's decision doesn't make sense to you. Sometimes, internal pressure. Sometimes, plain old exhaustion.

Complaining rarely helps. It doesn't improve your skill. It doesn't change the drill. It doesn't make the day shorter. It only drains your energy and the energy of the people around you.

Choosing not to grumble doesn't mean you ignore your feelings. It means you learn to bring them to God first, instead of letting them spill onto everyone else.

Maybe you can tell Him, "Lord, I'm frustrated today. Help me give my best anyway." Or, "I'm tired, but I want to honor You with my attitude."

Or, "Help me stay focused instead of complaining."

God meets you in that honesty. He strengthens your heart so you can show up with purpose even when you feel worn out.

Arguing is another challenge. In sports, disagreements happen daily about plays, calls, roles, expectations, decisions, and mistakes.

Constant arguing turns a team into a group of individuals competing against each other instead of alongside each other. Arguing closes your ears. It blocks learning. It turns simple correction into conflict.

When Paul warns against arguing, he isn't telling you to never speak up. Healthy communication matters. Asking questions matters. Clarifying instructions matters.

Arguing is different. Arguing fights to win. Arguing raises volume instead of understanding. Arguing pushes others away instead of inviting teamwork.

A mature athlete learns when to speak, when to listen, and when to let something go.

Avoiding grumbling also trains your heart in gratitude. Gratitude doesn't deny hard things, it simply notices the good things too. Even on difficult days, there are reasons to be grateful: the chance to play, the teammates around you, the people who drive you to practices, the ability to move your body, and the small improvements you don't always acknowledge.

Gratitude softens the instinct to complain.

And when your mind shifts, your atmosphere shifts.

Choosing not to grumble is not about pretending things are easy. It's about recognizing that God can grow you in hard moments. Some of your greatest maturity develops during days that push you. The way you respond to those days says more about your character than your stats ever will.

This verse also protects your influence. Younger athletes watch how you respond when things don't go your way. Teammates notice whether you complain or stay steady. Coaches pick up on your posture. Your attitude teaches others how to handle pressure, even when you don't realize anyone is watching.

Here's something to remember: you won't get this right every day. You will complain sometimes. You will argue. You will feel frustrated. You will say something you regret. None of that means you're failing. It just means you're human.

What matters is that you grow.

After a moment of grumbling, you can reset. After a heated reply, you can apologize. After a tough day, you can reflect and ask God for a steadier spirit tomorrow. Growth is not perfection. Growth is progress—slow, steady, day-by-day progress.

If you want a practical way to live out this verse, try this simple exercise: Before practice, choose one thing you will refuse to complain about today. Just one. Maybe it's conditioning, or maybe it's a teammate. Perhaps it's a coach's instructions. At the end of the day, notice how your experience changes when you remove one channel of negativity.

Your heart will feel lighter. Your mind will feel clearer. Your performance may even improve, and others will notice.

When you choose gratitude instead of grumbling, patience instead of arguing, peace instead of drama, you shine: quietly, steadily, and powerfully.

Before your next practice or game, whisper this prayer: "Lord, help me work today without grumbling. Make my attitude reflect You."

Let that prayer guide your tone, your posture, and your reactions.

Because a complaint spreads quickly, but so does encouragement. A harsh word escalates tension, but a calm word restores peace. A grumbling heart drains strength, but a grateful one lifts everyone around it.

Shine like the athlete God made you to be. Shine through effort, humility, and a heart that chooses joy over frustration. These choices will shape you far more deeply than any scoreboard ever could.

Chapter 22

"Cast all your anxiety on Him because He cares for you." - 1 Peter 5:7

Anxiety is one of those things athletes rarely talk about out loud, but almost everyone feels. It shows up in small moments: a tight chest before a tryout, a racing mind before a big game, a shaky feeling when a coach corrects you, or that knot in your stomach after a mistake.

Sometimes, it's obvious. Sometimes, it hides behind a calm face, but it's there.

God isn't surprised by this. That's why He gave us this verse. It's short, but it carries a kind of comfort you can feel deep in your chest. *Cast all your anxiety on Him because He cares for you.*

Not some anxiety. Not only the big stuff. All of it.

God invites you to hand Him every worry, every fear, every pressure, because He cares.

Athletes like you carry pressure that people outside your sport may not understand. You care about your performance. You care about your team. You care about your coach's opinion. You care about improving. You care about not letting people down. When you care deeply about something, it's easy for anxiety to slide in quietly.

You have probably felt anxiety during drills, watching game-film, or before competitions. Maybe you felt that way during conditioning, or late at night when your mind just wouldn't stop racing. Anxiety can show up anywhere, pretty much any time, even on your best days.

Some try to push it away by pretending they don't feel it. Others try to control every detail so they won't mess up. Others keep the anxiety inside until it spills out in frustration or tears.

The Bible doesn't tell you to ignore anxiety or hide it or control it. It tells you to place it in God's hands. Cast the worry away from yourself.

Casting something away means releasing it or letting it go. Dropping something heavy off your shoulders, or even throwing it away from yourself.

That's what God invites you to do.

Think of a fisherman throwing a net far away from his boat. He doesn't toss it gently at his feet; he throws it outward. That's the picture in this verse. Your anxiety doesn't belong trapped inside your chest. God wants you to throw it onto Him, completely and without fear of judgment.

He can handle what you cannot.

For young athletes, anxiety often shows up as questions:

"What if I'm not good enough?"

"What if I mess up?"

"What if Coach is disappointed?"

"What if I lose my spot?"

"What if everyone expects too much from me?"

These questions build pressure like stacking weights on your shoulders. God answers all of them with one truth: *I care for you.*

He doesn't care for you because of your athletic performance. He doesn't care only when you succeed. His care is steady, present, deep, and unconditional. He loves you on days you shine and on days you struggle. That truth alone can loosen anxiety's grip.

This verse also teaches something about timing. Anxiety usually shows up in the future: what *might* happen.

God meets you in the present. He invites you to bring Him your unknowns, one at a time, moment by moment.

Imagine walking into practice already tense. What if, before stepping onto the field or into the gym, you whispered, "Lord, here's my worry.

Please carry it so I don't have to." That simple prayer creates space for peace.

You may still feel nervous. Your stomach might still flutter, but the weight begins to shift. Anxiety doesn't disappear instantly, but it becomes lighter when you refuse to carry it alone.

Sometimes, anxiety comes from comparing yourself to others: teammates who seem more confident, stronger, faster, or smarter. You might wonder where you fit. You might wonder if you measure up.

Comparison is a thief. It steals joy and confidence. It whispers lies. God calls you to cast even that anxiety on Him. He reminds you that your worth never depended on being better than someone else.

One of the hardest parts of anxiety is that it often feels embarrassing. You may think other athletes are fearless and wonder why you feel shaky.

The truth is, many players carry hidden worries. The strongest athletes are not those who never feel anxious, but those who know where to take their anxiety.

God isn't asking you to be fearless. He's asking you to trust Him with your fear.

Sometimes, anxiety shows up physically. You feel tired, distracted, or unfocused. Sometimes, it shows up emotionally, and you feel irritable or sad.

Sometimes, it shows up mentally, where you get stuck in a loop of negative thoughts. That doesn't mean something is wrong with you. It means you need support. And God himself is the first and best place to turn.

You can talk to Him about anything.

"Lord, I'm overwhelmed."

"Lord, I'm scared I'll disappoint people."

"Lord, I feel pressure I can't explain."

"Lord, help me breathe and trust You."

Your prayers don't need perfect wording. They just need honesty.

Casting anxiety on God doesn't mean you won't work hard. It means you stop letting fear control your effort. It means you practice freely instead of tensely. It means you compete with clarity instead of panic. It means you learn to breathe again when pressure rises.

This verse also connects anxiety with identity. God tells you to cast your anxiety *because He cares.* That is a statement of value. It means you matter. Not your stats. Not your speed. You. Your heart. Your life. Your well-being.

When anxiety tells you that you're alone, God says, "You're not."

When anxiety tells you that you might fail, God says, "My love for you doesn't change."

When anxiety tells you to worry, God says, "Give it to Me."

There is nothing too small for God to carry.

No fear is too silly.

No concern is too minor.

No pressure is too quiet.

He cares for you.

One helpful practice is this: when you feel anxiety rising, name it. "Lord, I'm anxious about this drill." "Lord, I'm anxious about my performance today." "Lord, I'm anxious about making a mistake." Naming it is the first step to releasing it.

Then, imagine placing that concern in God's hands. Picture yourself physically handing it over. It may sound simple, but it can steady your heart.

Over time, you'll notice a shift. You'll start responding to pressure with more peace. You'll handle corrections with less panic. You'll approach games with a calmer mindset. You'll find yourself breathing deeper, thinking clearer. Not because you became less anxious on your own, but because you learned to cast your anxiety on the One who cares.

Before your next practice or competition, take ten quiet seconds.

Close your eyes.

Breathe slowly.

Whisper, "Lord, I cast my anxiety on You."

Let that be enough.

God is gentle with anxious hearts. He never rushes you or shames you. He simply invites you, again and again, to place your worries into His strong hands.

So, cast your anxiety, every piece of it. He cares for you far more than you know.

Chapter 23

"The Lord is my shepherd; I lack nothing." - Psalm 23:1

Psalm 23 is one of the most well-known passages in the Bible, but it often feels distant to young athletes who live in a world of busy schedules, tight expectations, and constant movement. Shepherds, sheep, pastures, it all sounds ancient, but when you slow down and sit with the first line, it becomes surprisingly personal.

"The Lord is my shepherd."

Not just *a* shepherd, *my* shepherd.

Someone who guides. Someone who protects. Someone who leads with care, not pressure. Someone who knows the path even when you don't.

In sports, it's common to feel like you have to guide yourself. You make decisions about training, friendships, effort, attitude, and even future plans. Coaches guide you too, but they can only see part of you. They see your performance.

God sees your heart. Coaches know your stats. God knows your fears, your dreams, your frustrations, your personality, your pace, and what will truly shape you.

When David wrote this psalm, he wasn't describing a distant God. He was describing a God who stays close, closer than you stay to your own thoughts. Shepherds walk beside their sheep, not behind them shouting instructions. They lead gently. They know the terrain. They spot danger before the sheep notice anything is wrong.

This is exactly how God leads you.

A young athlete often feels pressure to have everything planned out.

What position should I play?

What goals should I set?

What if I'm not improving fast enough?

What if others pass me?

What if I make the wrong choice?

When God is your shepherd, you're not expected to know the whole path. You're expected to follow the One who does.

"I lack nothing." This part of the verse can feel confusing. You might think, "But I don't have everything I want. I don't have perfect games. I don't always feel confident. I don't always understand what God is doing."

David isn't saying you'll never face hard days. He's saying God provides what you need, strength for your weakness, peace for your anxiety, rest for your tired heart, wisdom for your decisions, and protection in moments you don't even recognize as dangerous.

Think about a season when you felt stretched. Practices felt long. School felt overwhelming. Your emotions felt unstable. You pushed yourself, but still felt behind. During those times, you may have felt like you were lacking something: energy, clarity, confidence, or direction.

God stayed steady. Even when you didn't notice, He held you together.

When a shepherd guides sheep, the sheep don't always understand the path. They don't know where the green pastures are. They don't know where danger hides. They don't know which direction leads home, but the shepherd does. The sheep only need to stay close.

This psalm invites you to stay close.

Young athletes often chase so many things at once: approval, success, improvement, perfection, affirmation, a sense of belonging. These things are not wrong, but they can become exhausting when you try to hold them on your own. God offers something better: the assurance that you are cared for, guided, and provided for.

If the Lord is your shepherd, then you are not alone: not in fear, not in failure, not in confusion, not in pressure, not in waiting.

Shepherds don't run ahead and leave the sheep behind. They move at a pace the sheep can handle. God does that with you. He never rushes your growth. He never expects you to mature instantly. He never demands perfection. He leads you step by step, season by season.

This matters in sports because athletes often feel like they should grow faster. You want to master skills immediately. You want clear answers. You want to perform at your peak every day.

Growth doesn't happen in a straight line, spiritually or athletically. Some days feel strong. Some feel discouraging or confusing, but God is shepherding you through all of them.

Consider how He shepherds you:

He guides, giving quiet wisdom when you ask.

He protects, closing doors that would harm you.

He corrects, redirecting you when you drift.

He comforts, steadying your heart when fear rises.

He stays, never abandoning you, no matter the scoreboard.

A shepherd knows each sheep individually: its tendencies, strengths, weaknesses, and struggles. God knows you the same way. He knows your pace, your limits, your hopes, and your wounds. He knows when you need rest. He knows when you need encouragement. He knows when you need a challenge.

He knows when you need stillness.

If you're honest, there are probably areas in your life where you feel lost, not wildly lost, but quietly unsure. You may not know what your next steps are. You may feel uncertain about your role on your team. You may feel pressure to live up to someone's expectations. You may feel anxious about your future.

This verse reminds you that God is already walking ahead of you. The pressure to have everything figured out is not yours to carry. Your job is to follow. His job is to shepherd.

Following Him doesn't mean you lose freedom. It means you gain direction.

When God leads, peace grows, even in stressful seasons. Your decisions feel clearer. Your relationships become healthier. Your identity becomes steadier. You stop running after every source of approval because you already belong to the One who loves you as you are.

This doesn't mean your life will be perfect. Even shepherded sheep face storms, steep hills, and dark paths, but they walk through those places safely because they stay close.

If you want to experience God as your shepherd, start small:

Take a slow breath before practice and whisper, "Lead me, Lord."

Ask Him for wisdom before a difficult conversation.

Invite Him into moments when fear rises.

Trust Him when you feel unsure.

Lean on Him when your heart feels worn out.

These small habits build a shepherded life.

As you move through your season, wins, losses, highs, lows, remember that God's presence is not something you earn. It's something He gives freely because He cares deeply for you.

If the Lord is your shepherd, then you are not wandering.

You're being led.

You're being held.

You're being guided toward good things, even when you can't see them yet.

Before you step into your next game or practice, take a quiet moment and pray, "Lord, be my shepherd today." Trust that He will.

Because with Him guiding your steps, you truly lack nothing.

Chapter 24

"Your word is a lamp to my feet and a light to my path." - Psalm 119:105

There's a moment before almost every sports season when things feel unclear. It could be that you're unsure about your role, or wondering what your coach expects.

Maybe you're trying to figure out how to handle a new level of competition. Or maybe life outside of sports feels confusing, and it's hard to know which direction to take next.

In times like these, this verse from Psalm 119 feels especially steady. *"Your word is a lamp to my feet and a light to my path."*

Not a spotlight. Not stadium lights. Not a full map of everything ahead. A lamp.

A lamp only shows you the next few steps. It doesn't give you the entire route. It doesn't reveal every twist, turn, or challenge waiting ahead. It simply gives you enough light for right now.

For young athletes, who often want clear answers right away, this can be hard to accept. You want to know where your effort is leading. You want to know how things will turn out. You want clarity, certainty, and confidence.

God rarely gives the full picture in advance. Instead, He gives His Word, and His Word guides you, step by step.

If you've ever tried walking in the dark, you know how much difference a small light makes. Even a dim lamp gives you enough to move safely without stumbling. That's what God's Word does. It doesn't always tell you everything, but it tells you enough to move forward without fear.

So, what does it look like for Scripture to be a lamp for an athlete?

It means God's Word steadies your identity when the world tries to shake it.

It means God's Word keeps your heart calm when pressure rises.

It means God's Word helps you respond with wisdom instead of emotion.

It means God's Word gives you courage when doubt whispers too loudly.

It means God's Word keeps your steps aligned with who He is shaping you to be.

Sometimes, athletes look for guidance in a thousand different places: opinions, social media, comparisons, praise, criticism, or their own emotions.

Scripture gives something those sources never can: truth that doesn't shift with the day.

Think about the times you've felt confused or disappointed. Maybe you worked hard but didn't get the result you expected. Maybe someone else got the attention you hoped for. Maybe you felt left out. Maybe you were unsure whether you should keep pushing or slow down.

On days like that, you need something more reliable than your feelings. Your emotions can change in five minutes. God's Word does not.

Now, let's look at this verse again: *"a lamp to my feet."* It means Scripture helps you with the steps right in front of you: your attitude today, the choices you make this week, the way you treat people during practice, the way you handle disappointment, the way you respond to correction, the way you rest.

Scripture gives light for **today**, not only for your future.

The verse continues: *"a light to my path."* This means Scripture guides not just your present steps but also the direction of your life. It helps you form character that will carry you far beyond sports: integrity, honesty, humility, discipline, compassion, courage, and trust.

Young athletes sometimes think the Bible speaks only to "spiritual stuff," not sports.

God speaks to every part of your life, including the places where you compete, sweat, fail, succeed, and grow.

Here's an example:

When you struggle with fear, God's Word speaks to it.

When you wrestle with comparison, God's Word speaks to it.

When you face conflict, God's Word speaks to it.

When you're overwhelmed, God's Word speaks to it.

When you want to quit, God's Word speaks to it.

When you lose confidence, God's Word speaks to it.

When you celebrate a victory, God's Word shapes how you respond.

The Bible lights your path because it teaches you who God is, and when you know who He is, you walk differently.

A lamp also teaches patience. You can't sprint ahead when you can't see far. You take measured steps. You stay close to the light. You trust that the next few feet will be enough.

This is the opposite of how many young athletes feel. You want to leap ahead. Master the skill right now. Understand the plan right now. Know the future right now.

Spiritual growth and athletic growth happen step by step.

The lamp teaches you to slow your heart, pay attention, and trust the process.

There may be days when Scripture feels quiet. Days when you read it and nothing seems to stand out. Days when you're tired, distracted, or unsure what to pray. That doesn't mean the lamp isn't working.

Sometimes, the lamp simply keeps you from stepping into trouble. Sometimes, it steadies your mind without you noticing. Sometimes, it builds strength over time.

Think of training days when you don't feel like anything significant happened. You didn't set a record. You didn't have a breakthrough, but you still got better. Scripture works like that too. Not always dramatic, often steady and slow.

If you're unsure where to begin with reading the Bible, start small. A few verses before school. A short psalm before bed. A chapter on a quiet afternoon. The goal isn't to check a box, it's to let God's voice shape your day.

Ask simple questions as you read:

"What does this show me about God?"

"What might God be saying to my heart?"

"What step can I take today because of this?"

That's how a lamp works: small, steady light, one step at a time.

As you walk through your season, there will be days when things feel confusing. Days when your heart feels stretched. Days when you're unsure which direction to go. On those days, open Scripture. Even if you only read a few sentences. Let God's Word settle your thoughts and remind you that you are not walking alone.

Before your next practice or game, try praying:

"Lord, be the lamp for my feet today. Light my path."

You may not see everything clearly, but you will see enough.

Sometimes "enough" is exactly the blessing God wants to give you: light for the step you're on, guidance for the moment you're in, and peace in the truth that the One who lights your path also walks it with you.

Chapter 25

"Truly he is my rock and my salvation; he is my fortress, I will not be shaken.." - Psalm 62:6

There are moments in every athlete's life when everything feels shaky. It may be after a rough game, after a hard conversation with a coach, or during a week when nothing seems to go right.

Sometimes, the shakiness isn't about your sport at all, it's about friendships, school stress, or things happening at home. You try to stay steady, but your heart feels like it's standing on ground that keeps moving.

Psalm 62:6 speaks into that feeling with a strong, quiet confidence: *"Truly He is my rock and my salvation; he is my fortress, I will not be shaken."*

A rock doesn't move.

A rock doesn't give way.

A rock stays firm even when everything around it shifts.

That's the picture David is painting here. God does not change based on your mood, your performance, or your circumstances. He stays steady. Because He stays steady, you can learn to stay steady too.

Young athletes often try to anchor themselves in things that don't last: confidence, winning streaks, praise from others, starting positions, personal improvement. None of those things are bad, but they are not strong enough to hold your identity. They shift too easily. One mistake, one conflict, one setback, or one bad day can shake them.

God is different. He is your rock not just when life is good, but especially when life feels uncertain. He doesn't step away when pressure rises. He doesn't forget you when you feel small. He doesn't weaken when your confidence dips. He holds steady in every season of your life.

Because of that, you don't have to crumble every time something goes wrong. You don't have to fall apart when your plans fall apart. You don't have to panic when your circumstances feel shaky. You were meant to stand on something stronger than your own efforts.

"He is my fortress…"

A fortress is a place of protection. A place where you can catch your breath. A place where enemies lose their power. A place where you're surrounded by strength that isn't your own.

Many teenagers don't have a fortress, they have pressure instead. They sit with thoughts that feel heavy:

"What if I'm not good enough?"

"What if I disappoint someone?"

"What if I fall behind?"

"What if this is my fault?"

"What if I never improve?"

Those questions can shake your heart if you don't have somewhere safe to bring them. God wants to be that safe place. Not a hiding spot where you avoid life, but a stronghold where you are protected while you face it.

When David says, *"I will not be shaken,"* he isn't pretending his life is easy. He wrote those words while facing real fear, real danger, and real stress. His strength didn't come from ignoring hard things. His strength came from knowing who stood with him.

Your strength comes from the same place.

Think about a game where you felt off, even before it started. You knew something wasn't right. Your legs were heavy, or your thoughts were scattered, or your nerves got loud.

Somewhere in the back of your mind, you reminded yourself to breathe, to settle, to trust. That tiny moment of calm didn't come from forced confidence. It came from anchoring yourself in something steady.

That's what this verse invites you to do every day, not with fake strength, but with rooted strength.

God as your rock means:

You don't have to react to every negative thought.

You don't have to fall apart after one mistake.

You don't have to let fear run your decisions.

You don't have to let pressure speak louder than truth.

When God is your rock, you learn to stand firm even when emotions shift. You learn to stay calm even when situations feel unstable. You learn to breathe through tension instead of letting it control you.

Standing on a rock is a choice. You can know the truth but still let fear shake you. You can hear God's promises but still rely on your own strength. Stability doesn't come from information, it comes from trust.

Trust takes practice.

Trust grows slowly.

Trust deepens the more you lean on God in the small moments.

It could be choosing to pray for a few seconds before practice.

It could be reminding yourself that God loves you even on rough days.

It could be letting go of a mistake instead of replaying it in your mind.

It could be thanking Him for strength when you feel drained.

These small acts of trust build a strong foundation.

Another thing about rocks: storms don't move them. Wind doesn't break them. Rain doesn't wear them down. When your life sits on God, storms stop defining you. They may shake your circumstances, but they can't shake your identity.

As an athlete, you will face many storms: pressure, fatigue, self-doubt, unfair situations, sudden changes, and moments where confidence collapses. If God is your rock, those storms become moments where strength grows. Not because you are strong, but because He is.

Imagine approaching your next challenge with the quiet assurance:

"I may feel nervous, but God is my rock."

"I may feel pressure, but God is my fortress."

"I may feel unsure, but God holds me steady."

"I will not be shaken, because He is with me."

That kind of confidence cannot be faked. It comes from a deep place inside you, a place shaped by God's presence.

Before you step into whatever waits for you today, practice, a game, school, or even a difficult conversation, pause for a moment and breathe.

Say something simple, like: "Lord, be my rock today. Keep me steady."

Let that truth settle your heartbeat.

Let it settle your thoughts.

Let it remind you that you stand on something that cannot move.

You will face challenges in your sport and your life, but you do not face them unprotected. You face them with a fortress. With a rock beneath your feet. With a God who holds your life steady when everything else feels uncertain.

He began a good work within you.

He strengthens you.

He surrounds you.

He never leaves you.

With Him, you can stand firm.

With Him, you can breathe calmly.

With Him, you can face your next step with confidence.

You may feel shaken at times, but you do not have to live shaken.

God is your rock.

Stand on Him, and you'll find your strength again.

Chapter 26

"Wait for the Lord; be strong and take heart and wait for the Lord." - Psalm 27:14

Waiting is one of the hardest things a young athlete ever has to do. You train, you push, you hope, you plan, and then you face a stretch of time when nothing seems to move. You don't see progress. You don't get the result you prayed for. You feel stuck in a place between "not yet" and "I wish it were already here."

Psalm 27:14 speaks directly into that space.

Wait for the Lord.

Not wait aimlessly.

Not wait hopelessly.

Wait for Him with strength, with courage, and with trust.

These words carry a kind of strength that doesn't look dramatic on the outside but feels deep on the inside. Waiting is not a weakness. Waiting is a kind of quiet bravery.

Many athletes struggle with waiting because so much of your life feels urgent. You want answers now. You want improvement now. You want clarity now.

God often works through seasons that move slower than you prefer. Not to frustrate you, but to shape you.

Waiting is part of your training.

Think about the times in sports when waiting is necessary.

You wait for a starting whistle.

You wait for your turn in a drill.

You wait for the play to develop.

You wait to heal after an injury.

You wait to earn trust.

You wait to grow.

None of those moments mean you're failing. They mean the right moment hasn't come yet.

The same is true with God.

When David wrote this psalm, he wasn't sitting in comfort. He was facing pressure, fear, and uncertainty. Yet he chose to trust that God's timing was better than his own. He chose to believe that waiting was not wasted.

Waiting becomes easier when you understand who you're waiting *for.*

You are waiting for a God who sees you clearly.

A God who doesn't overlook your effort.

A God who knows your pace.

A God who understands what you need before you ask.

A God who strengthens you as you wait.

He is not slow. He is precise.

Young athletes often think delay means disappointment, but with God, delay often means development. While you're waiting, your heart grows. Your patience grows. Your courage grows. Your commitment grows. Sometimes the thing you're waiting for is less important than the person you become while waiting.

Think about a season when you wanted something so badly: a certain position, a certain outcome, a certain breakthrough. When it didn't happen right away, frustration rose. You wondered if something was wrong with you. You wondered if you were falling behind. You wondered if God heard your prayers.

Looking back, there are probably moments when God answered at the right time, not your time. Maybe you weren't ready earlier. Maybe the opportunity needed to shift. Maybe your confidence needed to grow. Maybe God wanted you to rely on Him instead of your own strength.

Waiting teaches dependence. It takes the pressure off your performance and places your focus on God's faithfulness. When you stop trying to force your own timing, you free your heart to rest.

The verse also says, "be strong and take heart." Waiting isn't passive. It's not sitting with folded hands, hoping something magically changes. It's showing up with steady faith even when you don't see progress yet.

Strength during waiting looks like:

Continuing to practice even when you feel discouraged.

Treating teammates well even when your heart is heavy.

Keeping your focus even when your role is unclear.

Praying even when answers feel slow.

Holding onto hope when doubt whispers loudly.

Taking heart means you don't quit on yourself or on God just because the path feels slow.

God uses waiting to build spiritual endurance. Physical endurance grows when you keep moving through fatigue. Spiritual endurance grows when you trust God through uncertainty.

Waiting also protects you. Sometimes what you want right now could damage you if you received it too soon. A bigger role, more responsibility, a higher level of competition.

These things require character strong enough to hold them. God strengthens you through waiting so you can carry what's coming.

There's another side to waiting: learning to stop controlling things that were never yours to control. Athletes often try to manage every detail, every rep, every drill, every outcome.

Control is exhausting. It creates anxiety. It feeds fear. Waiting teaches you to breathe again. It teaches you to trust that God knows what to do with your future.

During long stretches of waiting, you might feel God is silent. You might think nothing is happening.

Remember: Seeds grow underground before anyone sees them. Muscles strengthen while you rest. Healing happens quietly. Growth often starts in places no one notices.

That is how God works in your heart.

If you're waiting right now, waiting for clarity, waiting for confidence, waiting for an opportunity, waiting to feel like yourself again, this verse is for you. God is not ignoring you. He is guiding you in a pace meant for your good.

Before your next practice or school day, try praying,

"Lord, help me wait with a strong heart."

Not, "Hurry up, God."

Not, "Make everything easy."

Just, "Help me wait with strength."

You may not feel different instantly, but over time, you'll notice a shift. Your heart won't panic as quickly. You won't compare yourself as much. You'll make decisions with more peace. You'll see setbacks through a steadier lens. That's the fruit of waiting well.

Waiting with God builds trust.

Trust builds courage.

Courage creates peace.

Peace changes the way you approach every part of your life, including your sport.

So, wait for the Lord.

Not with fear, but with steadiness.

Not with frustration, but with hope.

Not with doubt, but with courage.

God is working, even in the silence.

Even in the stillness.

Even when you don't feel movement yet.

Your next step will come at the right time.

Until then, wait with a strong heart.

Chapter 27

"Do not be wise in your own eyes; fear the Lord and shun evil.." -
Proverbs 3:7

Every athlete eventually faces a time when confidence turns into pride. It usually happens quietly. You might have a few strong practices, get praise from your coach, see your stats go up, or finally beat someone you used to struggle against. It's normal and healthy to feel proud of your progress.

Sometimes, that pride changes. You might start to think you don't need advice, ignore corrections, or stop listening as carefully. You begin to depend more on yourself and less on God.

Proverbs 3:7 steps right into that inner shift: *"Do not be wise in your own eyes; fear the Lord and shun evil."*

It's not telling you to doubt yourself. It's not telling you to stay small or quiet. It's not telling you to ignore the gifts God placed inside you. It's reminding you that true wisdom comes from humility, and humility begins with seeing yourself clearly: your strengths, yes, but also your limits.

Athletes hear a lot of messages that encourage the opposite.

"Trust yourself first."

"You know what's best."

"You don't need anyone's help."

"Do whatever feels right to you."

Those sayings sound empowering, but they can lead you down strange paths. When you believe your own perspective is the only one that matters, you close the door to growth. You ignore the voices that God placed in your life: coaches, mentors, teammates, parents, and most importantly: Him.

Being "wise in your own eyes" isn't about being brilliant. It's about being stubborn.

It's about assuming you already know enough.

It's about resisting correction because it stings your pride.

It's about brushing off advice because you want to stay in control.

Humility creates space for wisdom.

Think about a moment when a coach corrected you in practice. Maybe it annoys you at the moment, and you probably thought something along the lines of, *"I already know what I'm doing."*

Later, that correction helped you improve. Maybe it saved you from a mistake you would've repeated. Maybe it gave you insight you didn't realize you needed.

Humility lets you learn from what you couldn't see on your own.

God often teaches you through the words of others. When you're humble, you hear Him more clearly. When you're proud, your ears close. The verse says to *fear the Lord,* which doesn't mean to be scared of Him. It means to honor Him, to recognize that His wisdom is greater than yours. When you fear the Lord, you trust His guidance, even when it challenges your comfort.

Athletes who grow the most aren't the ones who think they know everything.

They're the ones who stay teachable.

They're the ones who listen.

They're the ones who are quick to ask questions.

They're the ones who don't mind correction because they know it shapes them.

Humility is strength, not weakness.

"Shun evil" might seem like a strong phrase, but it captures something important. Pride leads to choices that hurt you. When you rely only on yourself, it becomes easier to justify selfish decisions:

cutting corners

speaking harshly

blaming others

ignoring conviction

hiding mistakes

seeking attention instead of truth

Those choices don't feel dramatic in the moment. They're small, but over time, they bend your heart away from God.

Humility protects you from that drift. When you fear the Lord, when you honor Him with your thoughts, decisions, and attitude, you naturally turn away from what harms you. You start to recognize when your motives aren't right. You start to feel uncomfortable when arrogance slips in. You begin to sense the difference between confidence and pride.

Confidence says, "I know God gifted me, and I'll use my gifts well."

Pride says, "I don't need God. I don't need correction. I know best."

The difference matters. One leads you forward. The other eventually leads you into trouble.

Consider some of the top athletes you look up to. Many say they keep learning, even after reaching great success. They surround themselves with people who keep them accountable and learn from their mistakes. These athletes succeed because they stay open to advice, not because they think they know it all.

God calls you into that same posture, not only in your sport, but also in your faith.

When was the last time you invited God into your decisions?

When was the last time you paused to ask what He wanted, instead of trusting your first instinct?

When was the last time you let Him correct a habit or attitude that wasn't healthy?

Humility starts with those quiet choices.

"Do not be wise in your own eyes" doesn't mean you can't have opinions or instincts. It means you're willing to hold them loosely in the presence of God's wisdom. It means you see your strength as a gift, not something you earned alone. It means you're open to being shaped.

Even Jesus lived this way. He didn't rely on His own voice alone. He listened to His Father. If Jesus demonstrated humility, why would we think we can grow without it?

As you continue in your sport, you'll face moments when pride whispers to you: "You don't need help."

"You know better than they do."

"You're fine on your own."

"Don't let anyone tell you what to change."

Those whispers sound appealing, but they weaken your foundation. They isolate you. They cut you off from the very wisdom that could propel you forward.

Humility does the opposite. It brings you closer to God. It clears your mind. It softens your heart. It strengthens your character. It frees you from pretending you have everything figured out.

Before your next practice, take a moment to pray something simple:

"Lord, give me a humble heart. Help me listen. Help me learn."

You may be surprised by how that posture changes everything, how conflicts shrink, how stress lightens, how your relationships improve, how your confidence becomes steadier because it's no longer built on your own understanding.

Humility doesn't lower you.

It lifts you.

It opens you to wisdom, peace, and maturity that pride can never provide.

Let God be your guide.

Let Him shape your thoughts.

Let Him lead you away from confusion and into clarity.

Because when you stop being "wise in your own eyes," you make room for the One whose wisdom never fails.

Chapter 28

"The Lord is close to the brokenhearted and saves those who are crushed in spirit." - Psalm 34:18

There are moments in an athlete's life that hurt more than you expect.

A season that falls apart.

A role you wanted but didn't receive.

An injury that takes you out right when things are improving.

A mistake that still echoes in your mind.

A friendship that shifts.

A disappointment you keep replaying when the lights are off and the day is quiet.

These moments break something inside you. Not loudly. Not dramatically. More like a slow crack that appears when pressure has been sitting on the same spot for too long. You don't always know how to talk about it. Sometimes you try to push through it. Sometimes you feel guilty for even struggling, but God sees what others miss.

"The Lord is near to the brokenhearted."

Near. Not distant. Not watching from far away. Near.

Those words hold a quiet comfort you might not realize you need until you're in the middle of a difficult moment. God doesn't wait for you to feel strong before He comes close. He doesn't show up only after you fix yourself. He draws near in the exact places you feel cracked, tired, discouraged, or defeated.

Brokenhearted moments are part of being human, even for young athletes who try to look strong on the outside. Your heart takes hits long before your body ever does. Sometimes, the emotional bruises hurt more than the physical ones.

The world around you often expects you to "shake it off." Teammates move on quickly. Coaches keep the schedule moving. Friends don't always understand. Everyone else seems fine, so you tell yourself you're fine too.

God does not rush you through pain. He meets you in it. He sits with you in it. He listens to what you can't explain to anyone else.

This verse also says God "saves those who are crushed in spirit."

A crushed spirit doesn't always look dramatic. Sometimes, it looks like a kid smiling on the outside while their chest feels heavy. Sometimes, it looks like silence: long, quiet silence. Sometimes, it looks like you're losing interest in things you used to enjoy. Sometimes, it looks like trying harder and harder to cover the ache.

God sees past the mask. He knows when your spirit feels flat, tired, or empty. He doesn't label you weak for it. He responds with compassion.

Think about a moment when your heart felt broken in a small or big way. Maybe you blew a chance in a game. Maybe a coach's words cut more deeply than they realized. Maybe a friend shifted away. Maybe someone made you feel invisible. Perhaps pressure built until you didn't know what to do with it.

You probably felt alone at that moment. Most people do, but this verse reminds you: *you were never alone.* God was near, closer than you knew.

Sometimes, God's nearness feels like peace in the middle of tears.

Sometimes, it feels like a sudden breath of calm.

Sometimes, it feels like a thought that brings hope.

Sometimes, it feels like strength returning slowly.

Sometimes, it feels like the courage to get up again.

Sometimes it feels like someone reaching out at the exact right time.

His presence doesn't always remove the pain instantly, but it carries you through it.

Athletes often try to keep emotions out of their sport, but God never asks you to hide your heart. He wants you to bring it to Him: your disappointment, your confusion, your sadness, your fears. He doesn't treat any of it as "too much."

Being brokenhearted is not a sign that your faith is small. It's a sign that you're human. David, who wrote this psalm, was a warrior and a king, a strong man by every measure.

He admitted that his heart broke sometimes. Instead of pretending he was okay, he reached for God.

You can too.

What does it look like to invite God into your brokenhearted moments?

It might look like praying, "Lord, this hurts. Please stay close."

It might look like reading a psalm when you don't have words of your own.

It might look like sitting in silence and letting tears fall.

It might look like asking God for comfort even when you don't understand why something happened.

It might look like whispering His name when you feel overwhelmed.

You don't have to pray perfectly. You don't have to know what to say. Honest prayers, even messy ones, reach God's heart.

Being brokenhearted also opens a path to deeper strength. Not the kind of strength that hardens or shuts people out. The kind that grows compassion. When you've been hurt, you notice when others might be hurting too. You become gentler. You become more aware. You see people with new eyes. You understand what it feels like to carry weight silently, so you choose kindness more often.

God can use even your broken moments to shape you into someone who reflects Him more clearly.

He never rushes your healing. Think of how injuries heal: slowly, quietly, steadily. Your heart needs time too. Some days you'll feel better. Some days the ache returns. Healing rarely moves in a straight line. But God walks with you through every part of it.

Here's something many athletes forget: God does not love you more on your strong days than He does on your weak ones. His nearness is not based on performance. He doesn't draw close only when you succeed. He draws close when you break.

Before your next practice or game, take a quiet moment and breathe deeply.

Tell God whatever sits heavy in your chest, even if it feels simple or small.

Let Him near.

Let Him steady you.

Let Him lift your spirit slowly, gently, faithfully.

You do not heal alone.

You do not carry heartbreak alone.

You do not walk through disappointment alone.

The Lord is near. Right now. Right where your spirit aches.

He is already holding the pieces of your heart with more care than you can imagine.

Chapter 29

"He gives strength to the weary and increases *the power of the weak."* - *Isaiah 40:29*

Every athlete knows what it feels like to reach the end of themselves.

Your legs feel heavy.

Your lungs burn.

Your mind grows foggy.

Your motivation slips a little.

Your confidence shakes.

Sometimes, it's not even your body that feels tired, it's your heart. You're worn out from balancing everything. School. Practice. Expectations. Pressure. Roles. Responsibilities. Emotions you can't quite name. There's a kind of tiredness that sleep doesn't fix. It sits deeper.

Isaiah 40:29 speaks to that exact place. *"He gives strength to the weary..."*

Not to the perfect. Not to the ones who never slip. Not to the ones who pretend they're fine.

He gives strength to the weary, the ones who feel empty, stretched thin, or worn out.

This verse isn't about pushing harder. It's about receiving strength from a God who never runs out of it.

Many young athletes are used to performing through fatigue. You've heard phrases like "keep going," "push through," "don't quit," and in many situations, those words help build perseverance.

The deeper kind of strength, the kind that keeps your heart steady when circumstances shake you, doesn't come from grinding harder. It comes from God.

Physical strength fades. Emotional strength dips. Mental strength wavers. God's strength doesn't rise and fall. It remains steady, available, and strong enough to hold you up when your own strength fails.

Think back to a moment when you felt truly weary, not just tired from a workout, but drained. Maybe something didn't go the way you hoped. Maybe someone's words cut deeper than they realized.

Maybe you were disappointed in yourself. Maybe life outside your sport felt heavy. In moments like that, you need more than muscle. You need the strength only God can give.

God's strength often shows up in quiet ways.

A sense of peace in the middle of chaos.

A breath that steadies your thoughts.

A feeling of calm right before a hard moment.

A little spark of courage when you want to avoid something.

A renewed desire to get up and try again.

His strength is not always loud. Sometimes, it's as gentle as a thought that says, "I'm with you."

This verse also says God "increases the power of the weak." That means weakness doesn't frighten Him. It doesn't disappoint Him. It doesn't make Him pull away. Weakness attracts His help. When you finally admit, "I don't have this today," God meets you with grace instead of judgment.

Athletes often hide their weakness because they want to appear tough. You push through pain, pretend you're fine, or act like nothing gets to you.

God invites honesty. Telling Him you're weary isn't failure, it's faith. It's saying, "Lord, I can't carry this on my own."

That's exactly where He meets you.

Isaiah wrote this chapter to people who felt discouraged, exhausted, and uncertain about their future. God didn't respond with frustration. He responded with reassurance, reminding them that He is strong enough for all the places they are weak.

This matters for your spiritual life, but it also matters for your sport. When God strengthens you, you gain something deeper than energy. You gain perspective. You begin to see moments of strain not as signs to quit, but as places where God can shape you.

There are a few ways God gives strength:

He strengthens you through His presence.

Sometimes, simply knowing God is near gives you courage to face a hard day. His presence calms the panic that tries to rise in your chest.

He strengthens you through His Word.

Scripture steadies your mind when doubt or fear tries to rule your thoughts.

He strengthens you through rest.

God created rest for a reason. You're not less committed when you rest; you're wiser.

He strengthens you through people.

A teammate's encouragement, a coach's kindness, a friend's support. These are ways God pours strength into you.

He strengthens you through endurance.

Each time you keep going with His help, your capacity grows.

Before God strengthens you, He usually invites you to slow down inside. Athletes are used to powering through. Slowing down feels unnatural.

God does His best strengthening work when you pause long enough to breathe.

Picture yourself in the middle of a practice where everything feels heavy. Your legs drag. Your confidence dips. You feel frustration, maybe even embarrassment. In that moment, many athletes fall into one of two traps:

They push so hard they break down emotionally. Or they give up and shut down completely.

What if you took a breath and prayed,

"Lord, I'm weary. Please strengthen me."

Not dramatic.

Not complicated.

Just honest.

God honors that kind of honesty.

His strength doesn't always remove the challenge. Sometimes, it simply helps you face it with a healthier heart. You may still have to run the drill. You may still have to face the team. You may still have to confront the frustration, but you won't be facing it alone.

Sometimes, God's strength shows up after the moment. You make it through something that felt impossible, and only later do you realize, "I shouldn't have had the energy for that. God carried me."

This verse also teaches a powerful truth: God's strength doesn't compete with your weakness, it fills it. You don't have to pretend to be strong enough. You don't have to mask your fatigue. You don't have to tough everything out on your own.

Your job is to bring your weakness to God. His job is to strengthen you.

When you get to the end of yourself, you've reached the beginning of His strength.

Your weakness is not the end. Your weariness is not a sign you're failing. It's a sign you need God, and needing Him is never a flaw.

Before your next practice or game, pause for ten seconds.

Close your eyes.

Take a breath.

Whisper, "Lord, give me strength today."

Let Him meet you in your tired places.

Let Him fill your empty places.

Let Him steady you when your spirit feels shaky.

He gives strength to the weary. Not once. Not occasionally. Continuously.

Let Him give that strength to you.

Chapter 30

"The Lord will fight for you; you need only to be still." - Exodus 14:14

There are moments in an athlete's life when the battle feels bigger than anything happening on the field or court. Moments when the pressure inside you is heavier than the weight of any opponent. Moments when doubt grows louder than your confidence. Moments when you feel outmatched, overwhelmed, or worn down in ways you didn't expect.

In Exodus 14, the Israelites stand trapped—an army behind them, a sea in front of them. They have no plan, no strength left, and no idea how they're supposed to move forward. Fear fills their voices. Panic rises. Everything seems impossible.

Then Moses says something surprising: *"The Lord will fight for you; you need only to be still."*

Still? When danger is real? When pressure is high? When fear is rising?

Stillness feels backwards. It feels weak. It feels passive.

Moses isn't telling them to give up. He's telling them to step back so they can see that the battle isn't theirs alone.

Many young athletes live as though every fight in their lives depends on their own strength. You may feel that if you don't control every detail, everything will fall apart. So, you push harder. You think more. You worry more. You try to handle situations that were never yours to carry.

This verse stops that cycle with one powerful truth: **God fights for you.**

Not instead of you working hard, but alongside you, overseeing the things you can't see, handling the things you can't control.

It doesn't mean you stop training, stop preparing, or stop caring. It means you stop assuming everything depends on you alone.

Think of the "battles" you face as an athlete:

A season full of ups and downs.

Competition for a position.

A coach's expectations.

Injuries.

Self-doubt.

Fear of mistakes.

Worries about the future.

Pressure to perform.

Conflicts on a team.

Comparison with teammates or opponents.

Some of these battles happen outside you, but many happen inside you. The internal ones often feel harder.

This verse becomes a lifeline in those moments.

"The Lord will fight for you."

He steps into the places you feel weak.

He stands in the places you feel unsure.

He holds the pieces you can't carry.

He defends your heart.

He guides your steps.

He fights battles you don't even recognize yet.

"Be still" doesn't mean ignoring your responsibilities. It means calming your heart long enough to remember who God is. It means choosing trust instead of panic. It means pausing the frantic voice inside you and replacing it with truth.

Stillness looks like:

Taking a breath before you respond.

Praying before you panic.

Letting go before you spiral.

Saying, "Lord, I give this to You," even when your hands shake.

For many athletes, the hardest battles happen at night, when the loud world quiets and your thoughts rise. You replay your mistakes. You worry about tomorrow. You analyze everything. You try to solve problems that won't be solved by thinking harder.

God whispers the same words spoken to the Israelites:

I will fight for you.

You don't have to hold this alone.

That doesn't mean everything will be easy. God didn't snap His fingers and teleport the Israelites to safety. He made a path through the sea, a path they never imagined could exist. They still had to walk it, but God handled what they could not.

He did the impossible.

He opened the way.

He fought the enemy.

He cleared the path.

He carried them through.

There may be places in your life right now where you feel backed into a corner, unsure what to do next. Maybe it's your role on the team, or your confidence in that position. Maybe it's friendships. Maybe it's your future plans. Perhaps it's something painful you haven't told anyone.

You don't have to fix every piece by yourself. Bring it to God. Place your fear in His hands. The battle is His, not yours alone.

Sometimes God fights for you by giving you peace in situations that feel turbulent.

Sometimes He fights for you by giving you courage when you're afraid.

Sometimes He fights for you by shutting doors that aren't meant for you.

Sometimes He fights for you by opening opportunities no one could have predicted.

Sometimes He fights for you by strengthening you through struggle.

His fight doesn't always look loud. Sometimes, it looks calm when you expected panic. Sometimes, it looks like clarity when you expected confusion. Sometimes, it looks like steady growth when you expected collapse.

Stillness also protects you from fighting battles that drain you unnecessarily, like comparison, insecurity, or perfectionism. God never asked you to earn your worth. He simply asks you to walk with Him.

The Israelites could not split the sea by effort, planning, or strength. Only God could do that. The same is true in your life. There are parts of your journey that only God can move. When you try to force it, you feel frustrated. When you step back and trust, He guides.

Before your next practice or game, try this:

Find a quiet moment, even ten seconds.

Close your eyes.

Take one slow breath.

Pray, "Lord, I trust You. Fight for me today."

Let that be the anchor for your heart.

You are not fighting alone.

You never were.

You never will be.

When life feels overwhelming, when pressure grows, when battles rise around you or inside you, remember this promise: **God fights for you.** Not because you earned it, but because He loves you.

Let Him lead.

Let Him defend you.

Let Him clear the path.

Be still, because your God is great.

PART IV
Character Set:
Competing with Integrity

Chapter 31

"Nehemiah said, "Go and enjoy choice food and sweet drinks, and send some to those who have nothing prepared. This day is holy to our Lord. Do not grieve, for the joy of the Lord is your strength." - Nehemiah 8:10

There are days when being an athlete feels light and fun. You laugh through warmups, your body cooperates, your shots fall, your timing feels sharp, and everything seems to click. On those days, strength feels natural, almost effortless.

There are other days, and sometimes more of them than you'd like.

Days when your legs feel heavy.

Days when emotions cloud your focus.

Days when nothing goes right, no matter how hard you try.

Days when pressure builds, and joy seems far away.

It's on those days that this verse speaks the loudest:

"The joy of the Lord is your strength."

Not your talent.

Not your mood.

Not your confidence.

Not your circumstances.

His joy.

For many, the idea of joy feels tied to performance and good results. You feel joy after a good game. You feel joy when people notice and comment on your improvement, and when your coach praises you. Joy becomes something earned rather than received.

The joy Nehemiah talks about isn't based on anything you achieve. It comes from God Himself. It flows from His character, His presence, His unchanging love. This joy is steady even when your emotions aren't. It stays rooted even on days when everything feels shaky.

To understand this verse better, think about what was happening in Nehemiah's time. The people had been through a long season of discouragement. They were tired. They were worn down. Some were grieving. Some felt guilty. Some felt overwhelmed. And right in the middle of all of that, Nehemiah told them that God's joy, not their effort, would make them strong.

Strength built on joy may sound strange at first, because joy is often mistaken for a feeling.

In Scripture, joy is more like an anchor. It's a deep, steady confidence in who God is: good, faithful, forgiving, present, loving, patient, steady. When that truth sinks into your heart, it strengthens you from the inside out.

Joy doesn't always look like a smile. Sometimes, joy looks like calmness during stress.

Sometimes joy looks like gratitude after a small win.

Sometimes joy looks like patience when you want to rush.

Sometimes joy looks like breathing slowly instead of panicking.

Sometimes joy looks like hope when circumstances look discouraging.

Joy is not loud. It's steady.

As an athlete, you face many moments that try to steal your joy: comparison, criticism, mistakes, pressure, exhaustion, doubt, conflict, and fear. When joy slips away, strength slips with it. You start playing tight. You get frustrated faster. You lose confidence. You forget who you are and who God is.

When joy returns, even a small spark of it, you rise. Something inside you becomes lighter. You compete with clearer eyes. You stop forcing things. Your heart steadies. Strength grows again.

That is why Nehemiah didn't say, "Find strength on your own." He said, "The joy of the Lord is your strength." The source is not you. And that's good news.

So, where do you actually find this kind of joy?

You find it by remembering God cares for you deeply.

Not because of your performance, but because you are His.

You find it by remembering God is with you in every setting: warmups, bus rides, quiet nights, stressful moments.

He doesn't step in and out.

You find it by noticing small blessings around you.

A kind teammate. A breakthrough in practice. A moment of encouragement. A cool breeze on a warm day. A chance to play at all.

You find it by letting go of the pressure to be perfect.

Joy grows when perfection stops ruling your heart.

You find it by talking to God, even about small things.

He listens, always.

Joy grows when you feel safe with God rather than judged by Him. Many young athletes picture God as someone who is pleased only when they perform well or disappointed when they mess up.

Scripture paints an entirely different picture. God sings over His children, rejoices in them, comforts them, carries them, and strengthens them.

Joy grows when you know you are loved.

This verse also helps you reframe discouragement. When you feel defeated, whether after a bad game, a tough practice, or a hard week, you don't have to pretend everything is fine. The people Nehemiah was speaking to weren't told to "cheer up." They were told not to stay in grief because God's joy was available to them.

You can be honest about your emotions while still anchored in truth.

"Yes, this is hard."

"Yes, I'm disappointed."

"Yes, today wasn't my best."

But also:

"God is still good."

"God still loves me."

"God is still with me."

"God still strengthens me."

Joy and sadness can exist in the same heart, but joy ultimately holds the stronger grip.

There's another layer to this verse: joy fuels resilience. Athletes often think grit comes from toughness.

Grit also comes from joy, the kind of joy that reminds you why you started playing in the first place. The kind of joy that helps you get back up. The kind of joy that refuses to let failure define you.

Joy keeps you steady under pressure.

Joy helps you respond to frustration with patience.

Joy opens your heart to learning instead of shutting down.

Joy helps you encourage others even when you're having a tough day.

Joy makes you a better teammate, because when joy fills you, kindness and support naturally overflow.

Joy also reconnects you to gratitude. It reminds you that playing is a gift, not a burden. Even hard days can hold purpose. Even tough drills can grow you. Even setbacks can teach you something valuable. Gratitude doesn't erase difficulty, but it reframes it.

Take a moment and think: When was the last time you felt joy in your sport, not because you won, but because you simply enjoyed playing?

That joy wasn't random. It was a gift.

God's joy steadies you the same way a coach's confidence steadies a team. When you know you have support, you play differently. When you know God delights in you, strength rises again.

Before your next practice or game, whisper this simple prayer: "Lord, fill me with Your joy today."

Let that prayer shift your mood.

Let it guide your thoughts.

Let it soften the pressure you're carrying.

Let it strengthen you in ways you didn't know you needed.

Because the joy of the Lord is not fragile.

It is strong.

It is steady.

It is yours.

Let His joy be your strength today, and every day ahead.

Chapter 32

"Let the peace of Christ rule in your hearts, since as members of one body you were called to peace. And be thankful." - Colossians 3:15

Pressure is a familiar feeling for young athletes. It shows up everywhere: before games, during tough drills, on the sidelines, in the locker room, in conversations with coaches, in the quiet moments before bed when your mind replays every mistake. Pressure whispers that you need to do more, be more, prove more, impress more.

Some days it feels like pressure, not peace, is ruling your heart.

Colossians 3:15 offers something very different: *"Let the peace of Christ rule in your hearts."*

Let it.

Let it take the lead.

Let it settle the noise.

Let it call the shots inside you.

Peace is not the absence of challenge. It's the presence of Christ, steady, calming, anchoring, right in the middle of it.

Many athletes think peace comes only when everything is going well. When your performance is solid. When the team is clicking. When a coach seems pleased. When you feel confident. Those moments are nice, but they're not the source of real peace. They're temporary. Circumstances rise and fall constantly.

Real peace, the kind Paul describes, goes deeper than emotion. It comes from a Person, not a moment.

Peace becomes your ruling force when Christ becomes the center of your heart.

To "rule" means to guide, direct, influence, steady, and interpret. In sports terms, it's like saying:

Let the peace of Christ be the referee of your heart.

Let His peace make the calls.

Let His peace decide what gets your attention and what doesn't.

Because if peace doesn't rule your heart, something else will: worry, fear, insecurity, comparison, perfectionism, frustration, or pride. And those things are terrible rulers. They stir chaos. They take your focus. They drain your joy.

Peace does the opposite.

Peace steadies.

Peace quiets.

Peace clears your mind.

Peace brings you back to what matters.

As an athlete, you will always face moments that try to shake you. A disappointing performance. A coach's hard feedback. A confusing role. A teammate who frustrates you. An unexpected mistake. A game that doesn't go your way. Each of these moments tries to rise up and rule your thoughts.

Scripture gives you a choice: Let Christ's peace be the voice that decides how you move forward.

This peace isn't passive. It actively shapes your reactions.

When pressure rises, peace says, "Breathe."

When doubt creeps in, peace says, "Remember who you belong to."

When frustration spikes, peace says, "Slow down."

When comparison tries to take over, peace says, "Stay in your lane."

When fear whispers, "You're going to mess up," peace says, "You're held by God."

Peace does not remove challenges. It helps you walk through challenges with confidence instead of panic.

Think about a moment when your heart felt scattered, when your thoughts ran in a hundred directions, and everything felt urgent. In that moment, imagine Christ's voice stepping into the chaos and saying, "Let My peace rule here." The rush fades. The noise quiets. Your heart steadies.

This is not imaginary. This is what Paul invites you into.

Peace also affects your physical performance. When your heart is ruled by stress, your muscles tighten, your breathing shortens, your confidence wavers, and your decision-making suffers.

When peace rules, your movements become smoother, your mind becomes clearer, and your presence becomes calmer. Peace helps you play freely instead of fearfully.

The verse begins with one important word: *"Let."*

That means peace is something you welcome. It doesn't force its way in. You open the door. You choose it. You make space for it.

So, how do you actually "let" Christ's peace rule?

You pause before reacting.

A deep breath can give peace room to speak.

You pray simple prayers throughout the day.

"Lord, calm my heart."

"Jesus, guide my thoughts."

"Give me Your peace right now."

You fill your mind with Scripture instead of fear.

A verse becomes a grounding place when emotions feel turbulent.

You release control.

Peace grows when you stop trying to manage everything alone.

You practice gratitude.

Thankfulness softens anxiety and opens your heart to God's presence.

You stay honest with God about your feelings.

Peace doesn't grow in hearts that pretend. It grows in open ones.

Peace also creates space for better relationships. When your heart is calm, you communicate more clearly. You listen better. You respond with patience instead of irritation. You bring steadiness to your team instead of tension. People feel safe around those who carry peace.

One of the biggest benefits of peace is clarity. When your heart is loud, you misread situations. A coach's correction feels like rejection. A teammate's stress feels like anger. A mistake feels like the end of the world.

When peace rules your heart, you see things accurately. You respond with wisdom instead of emotion.

Paul's instruction isn't about pretending pressure doesn't exist. It's about choosing who gets to define your internal world. Pressure can't rule you if peace does. Fear can't rule you if peace does. Failure can't rule you if peace does. Even success can't take over your heart when Christ's peace holds the highest place.

Here's something important: the peace Christ gives is stronger than your feelings. You may still feel nervous. You may still feel stressed. You may still feel uncertain. Peace doesn't erase emotion. It steadies you in the middle of it.

It's the difference between standing in a storm and standing in a storm *with a shelter over you.*

Christ's peace is your shelter.

Before your next practice, game, or stressful moment, try this:

Place your hand on your chest for a second and pray,

"Jesus, let Your peace rule here."

That simple act shifts your attention back to the One who carries you.

Let His peace be what guides you in the hard moments.

Let His peace calm your thoughts when pressure rises.

 Let His peace shape your reactions when emotions flare.

Let His peace remind you that you are safe in Him.

Because strength is good.

Effort is good.

Discipline is good, but without peace ruling your heart, those things become heavy.

Let Christ's peace be the steady center of your life, even on the hardest days.

Chapter 33

"He has shown you, O mortal, what is good. And what does the Lord require of you? To act justly and to love mercy and to walk humbly with your God." - Micah 6:8

Sports can bring out a wide mix of emotions, excitement, frustration, determination, disappointment, joy, and sometimes a level of intensity you didn't expect. One moment you feel proud of a great play, and the next you feel upset over something small. You see great teamwork, but you also see unfair behavior.

You experience encouragement, but you also see tempers flare. You see leadership, but you also notice arrogance. In the middle of all this, it can be hard to know how God wants you to carry yourself.

Micah 6:8 gives a clear, steady answer in just a few words: *"Act justly, love mercy, walk humbly with your God."*

It doesn't talk about talent.

It doesn't talk about winning.

It doesn't talk about being perfect.

It talks about character: the part of you that shapes everything else.

"Act justly."

Justice is simply doing what is right, even when it costs something. It means playing fair, even if you think no one is watching. It means owning mistakes instead of blaming others. It means treating people with the same respect you want from them. Acting justly isn't about being loud or dramatic. Often it's quiet. It shows up in choices others may overlook.

A teammate gets blamed for something that wasn't fully their fault. Acting justly means speaking up.

A player gets made fun of behind their back. Acting justly means stepping in or refusing to join.

You're tempted to cut corners in a drill. Acting justly means giving your full effort even when no one is grading you.

Justice is practical. It's small decisions that reveal what kind of person you're becoming.

"Love mercy."

Mercy is deeper than kindness. It shows up when someone doesn't deserve it or hasn't earned it. Mercy steps in when frustration wants to take over. Mercy chooses patience when impatience feels easier. Mercy gives someone another chance when your first instinct is to stay disappointed or annoyed.

You probably see mercy every week without realizing it. A coach pulls you aside to correct you instead of giving up on you. A teammate forgives you for something you said in anger. A friend understands that you were overwhelmed. Someone treats you gently on a day when you didn't explain how hard things felt.

You know how much mercy means when you receive it; God calls you to extend that same mercy to others.

This might look like not snapping back after someone's harsh comment during practice.

It might mean forgiving a teammate who messed up a play that cost you the win.

It might mean letting go of a grudge, not because it feels easy, but because bitterness only weighs you down.

Mercy frees your heart. It makes room for peace. It softens hard edges. And it mirrors the way God treats you, with patience, grace, and compassion.

"Walk humbly with your God."

Humility is one of the strongest qualities an athlete can have. It's not a weakness. It's not thinking poorly of yourself. It's simply knowing your strength comes from God and not letting pride cloud your heart. Humility keeps you grounded. It reminds you that your gifts are from Him. It helps you stay teachable, even when you're improving or receiving praise.

Walking humbly means recognizing that you still have growing to do. It means learning from correction instead of resisting it. It means not acting like you're better than teammates who aren't at your level yet. It means celebrating the success of others without feeling threatened. It means admitting when you're wrong and stepping forward with a calm spirit.

Humility also creates space for God to work in you.

Pride closes your ears.

Humility opens them.

Pride tries to take credit.

Humility gives credit to God.

Pride says, "I've got this alone."

Humility says, "God, stay with me."

Walking humbly is a daily choice, not a one-time decision. It shows up in your posture, your tone, your attitude, your reactions, and even the thoughts you don't speak out loud. Humility strengthens your relationships, deepens your faith, and steadies your spirit in high-pressure moments.

Micah 6:8 brings all three of these traits together: justice, mercy, and humility. When they work together, they shape your entire approach to life and sport. You become someone others trust. Someone teammates respect. Someone coaches rely on. Someone who carries themselves in a way that shines God's character without having to announce it.

God is not asking for perfection. He is asking for a willing heart.

Think back on this past week. Were there moments when you acted justly, or when you stayed quiet even though you knew you should've spoken up? Were there moments when you gave mercy, or when you let frustration win? Were there moments when humility guided you, or when pride tried to make decisions for you?

These reflections are not meant to shame you. They are meant to guide you. God doesn't point out areas of growth to bring you down—He points them out to help you rise.

Act justly.

Love mercy.

Walk humbly.

None of these come naturally, especially in competitive environments. That's why you need God. You're not asked to do these things alone. You're invited to walk with Him. Walking suggests movement, closeness, and step-by-step companionship. God doesn't give you a list and say, "Good luck." He says, "Let's do this together."

Before your next practice or school day, pause for a few seconds. Take a slow breath. Pray quietly: "Lord, help me act justly, love mercy, and walk humbly today."

Let that prayer settle your thoughts. Let it shape your reactions. Let it soften the places inside you that feel tight. Let it guide you in the moments where your emotions want to take over.

Character matters more than talent.

Mercy matters more than winning.

Humility matters more than attention.

These traits will stay with you long after your season ends. They will shape not just your sport, but your relationships, your decisions, your faith, and your future.

God has already given you everything you need to live this out. Walk with Him, step by step. He will guide you as you grow into the person He created you to be.

Chapter 34

"But those who hope in the Lord will renew their strength. They will soar on wings like eagles; they will run and not grow weary, they will walk and not be faint." - Isaiah 40:31

Some days as an athlete feel easy. Your body responds well, your mind is sharp, and everything falls into place.

There are many other days too: days when you wake up drained, days when you walk into practice already tired, days when pressure builds in a way you can't explain, days when your heart feels worn out even if your body seems fine. On those days, Isaiah 40:31 feels like a breath of fresh air.

Strength fades. Everyone feels it. Yet this verse promises that God gives strength in a way that renews you from the inside out, not through adrenaline or hype, but through hope. Hope in the Bible isn't wishful thinking. It's trust. It's confidence in who God is. It's leaning on His steady presence when yours feels shaky. It's placing your life into His hands and believing He holds you with care.

For many athletes, strength is something you try to produce on your own. You push harder. You train more. You grit your teeth and try to keep going. That approach works for a while, but eventually you'll run into a wall your effort cannot break. That wall might be fatigue, discouragement, fear, or a slow-burning exhaustion you can't shake. At that point, effort alone won't renew you. You need something deeper, something only God can give.

Isaiah writes that those who hope in the Lord "will renew their strength." That means your strength isn't meant to stay the same. God intends to refill what life drains. When you turn to Him, you're not asking for a small boost, you're asking for renewal, like a fresh start in the parts of you that feel worn thin.

The verse continues with the picture of soaring on wings like eagles. The beauty of this image is that eagles don't stay in the air by flapping wildly. They soar because they rise into the wind and let it lift them. Their strength isn't frantic; it's steady. Their height doesn't come from constant effort but from leaning into something stronger.

That's what it feels like when God lifts you. Life may still have storms, but you're not being tossed around by them. You rise above the fear, above the pressure, above the noise that once pulled you down. You see with clearer eyes. You move with calmer strength.

There are moments in your season when this kind of soaring feels impossible. Maybe you're discouraged about your performance, or frustrated with your role. Maybe you feel overlooked. Maybe pressure has taken the joy out of your sport.

Maybe life outside your sport is stretching you thin. Hope in God doesn't erase these challenges, but it gives you a way to rise through them instead of sinking under them.

Then the verse says you will run and not grow weary. That doesn't mean you'll never get physically tired. It means God's strength fills you in a way that keeps your heart steady. Weariness is different from tiredness. Tiredness comes from effort. Weariness comes from discouragement. Weariness feels like, "I don't know if I can keep doing this."

God renews your strength so the discouragement doesn't win. You keep going, not because you feel amazing, but because God carries you.

Athletes are familiar with pushing past tiredness. You know what it's like when your legs burn or your lungs feel strained.

Spiritual tiredness can feel even heavier than being physically worn out. It appears when your confidence drops, when your mistakes seem overwhelming, when pressure builds in your chest, or when you give your all but still feel like it's not enough. In those times, God gives you strength that doesn't depend on how you feel. He meets you in your weakness and gives you the courage to keep moving forward.

The verse ends with a quiet promise: you will walk and not faint. Sometimes, walking is the hardest part. Running gets attention. Soaring sounds exciting, but walking, just taking one step at a time, feels ordinary.

Most growth happens during seasons of walking. These are the days when you don't feel dramatic progress, when you aren't celebrating victories, when you're simply trying to stay faithful. God renews your strength in these seasons, too. You don't collapse. You don't fall away. You keep going with a steady heart.

Hope in the Lord changes how you move through every part of life. When your hope is in your performance, your strength rises and falls with each game. When your hope is in approval from others, your confidence rises and falls with their reactions. When your hope is in your own ability, pressure becomes unbearable. But when your hope is in God, your strength becomes rooted in Someone stable. You walk into every room, every drill, every challenge knowing you are not carrying yourself alone.

Hope is a daily choice. Some days it's easy. Other days, you have to whisper it with shaky hands. You choose hope when you wake up and pray, "Lord, give me strength for today." You choose hope when you step into practice feeling low but ask God to steady your heart.

You choose hope when you face discouragement and remind yourself that God sees you, knows you, and is working even when progress feels slow. You choose hope when you stop trying to control everything and trust that God guides the path you cannot see.

God never asks you to pretend you're strong. He asks you to bring Him your weakness so He can renew you. He doesn't expect perfection. He expects honesty. When you approach Him with an open heart, even a weary one, He fills you with strength that doesn't run out at the end of the day.

Before your next practice or game, pause for a moment and breathe deeply. Whisper, "Lord, renew my strength." Let that be your anchor. Let that simple prayer settle your heart. Let His presence lift you like the wind beneath an eagle's wings.

You don't have to soar on your own.

You don't have to run on empty.

You don't have to walk alone.

Hope in the Lord, and He will renew your strength: today, tomorrow, and every day ahead.

Chapter 35

"Cast your cares on the Lord and he will sustain you; he will never let the righteous be shaken." - Psalm 55:22

Every athlete carries burdens, even if no one sees them. Some burdens come from the sport itself, pressure to perform, fear of letting people down, frustration with your progress, disappointment after a tough game, or the weight of expectations you quietly place on your own shoulders.

Other challenges come from outside your sport, like stress from school, confusing friendships, family problems, or thoughts you keep inside because you're not sure anyone would understand.

You get used to carrying these things. You put on a confident face. You show up to practice. You compete hard. You act strong because you feel like that's what an athlete is supposed to do. Inside, the weight adds up. Even when you don't realize it, the pressure begins to drain your joy and tighten your spirit.

Psalm 55:22 meets you right in that place: *"Cast your burden on the Lord and He will sustain you."*

Many athletes struggle with this because they don't want to look weak. They fear that giving God the weight means admitting they can't handle everything.

That's exactly the point. You aren't built to handle everything. God is.

Some burdens are heavy and obvious, like an injury, a major disappointment, or a conflict that hurts your heart. Some burdens are quiet and hidden, like anxiety, self-doubt, loneliness, or the pressure to keep up with others. This verse covers all of them. God doesn't grade your burdens by size. If it weighs on you, He wants it.

Many athletes are good at pushing pain down. You keep moving, hoping the weight will shrink on its own. Burdens rarely shrink in silence. They grow. They press deeper. They show up in unexpected ways: snapping at someone, losing patience during practice, feeling discouraged after small mistakes, or lying awake replaying thoughts you can't quiet.

Casting your burden on God doesn't mean ignoring your problems. It means transferring them from your shoulders to His. It means you pray honestly:

"Lord, I can't carry this anymore."

"God, this situation feels too heavy."

"Father, take this pressure from me."

"Lord, hold what I cannot."

This kind of prayer isn't a weakness. It's strength wrapped in humility. It's strength that knows where to turn when your own runs out.

The verse continues: *"He will sustain you."*

Not *might.*

Not *sometimes.*

Not *if you impress Him.*

He **will** sustain you.

To sustain means to hold you up, support you, and give you enough strength for each step, one moment at a time. God doesn't promise to remove every burden instantly, but He promises to carry the weight of it so it doesn't crush you. He promises to walk with you so you don't face anything alone. He promises to give you rest when your heart feels tired.

Think about how you feel when someone helps you carry something heavy. The weight in your hands doesn't magically disappear, but suddenly, it feels lighter. Your body relaxes. Your steps feel different. You can breathe again.

That's what God does for your inner world. He takes the strain off your spirit so you can walk steady instead of stumbling under pressure.

Maybe your burden is pressure from a coach who pushes hard. Maybe it's the feeling that you're falling behind. Maybe it's a mistake that still bothers you. Maybe it's a friendship that changed unexpectedly.

Maybe it's a worry about the future. Maybe it's something you haven't told anyone because words don't feel big enough to describe it.

Whatever it is, God sees it, not as something small or silly, but as something He cares about deeply.

This verse also reminds you that God doesn't step away when you're struggling. He steps **closer**. He stays near when your heart is heavy. He listens when you don't have a clear sentence to offer Him. He understands the things you can't articulate. You don't have to sound impressive when you pray. You just have to be honest.

"Lord, here it is... please take this." That simple prayer reaches Him every time.

Casting your burden on the Lord also means giving Him the burdens you pick up by comparing yourself to others. Plenty of athletes carry the silent pressure of constantly measuring themselves against others: teammates, opponents, kids they see online.

Comparison is a heavy burden because it never ends. Someone always seems faster, stronger, or more confident. God doesn't ask you to carry the weight of being "better." He asks you to carry the weight of being faithful. He made you on purpose, with intentional gifts and a unique path. He calls you to walk *your* journey, not someone else's.

Another burden athletes often carry is the fear of making mistakes. Even small errors can feel overwhelming when you place your worth inside your performance.

God doesn't tie His love to your results. He doesn't pull away when you fall short. He sustains you, because He loves you deeply.

When you give Him your burden, you create space for peace to grow. Peace brings clarity. Peace loosens tension. Peace takes anxiety off the throne and replaces it with trust. Peace helps you breathe again.

The key phrase in the verse is "cast your burden." God won't rip the burden out of your hands. He waits for you to release it. He waits for your willingness. Strength grows when you choose surrender, not when you cling to pressure.

You might need to cast the same burden more than once. That's okay. Sometimes you release a worry in prayer, only to pick it up again later without noticing. God isn't annoyed by this. He invites you to cast it again, and again, until letting go becomes part of your rhythm.

Before your next practice or game, or even before school tomorrow, take a small moment and say quietly, "Lord, I cast my burden on You today."

Let those words settle.

Let your breath slow.

Let God lift the weight you've been carrying alone.

He will sustain you.

He will steady you.

He will give you enough strength for each step ahead.

You don't have to hold the entire world together.

Your job is to hand God the burden.

His job is to carry it.

He never fails at His part.

Chapter 36

"But he said to me, "My grace is sufficient for you, for my power is made perfect in weakness." Therefore I will boast all the more gladly about my weaknesses, so that Christ's power may rest on me." - 2 Corinthians 12:9

Every athlete eventually faces a moment when strength, talent, confidence, or energy just aren't enough. You try to ignore it, push harder, and tell yourself to toughen up. Still, deep down, you sense a limit you didn't see coming.

Most athletes dislike that feeling. Weakness can feel like failure, and falling short can seem final. You're used to solving problems with effort, discipline, or determination. But what happens when none of that works? What do you do when the challenge just won't move?

This verse gives an answer you may not expect: God meets you in weakness, not with frustration, but with grace.

When Paul wrote these words, he wasn't celebrating his strength. He was struggling. He had something in his life that weighed on him deeply, something he prayed about again and again. He wanted it gone. He wanted relief. He wanted to feel strong again.

God didn't remove the struggle. Instead, He spoke this promise: *"My grace is sufficient for you, for My power is made perfect in weakness."*

In other words:

You don't need to be strong for Me to work.

You don't need to hold everything together.

You don't need to pretend.

I will supply what you cannot.

For an athlete, this truth can feel both surprising and freeing. You spend so much of your life trying to prove you're strong: physically, mentally, emotionally.

God says His strength shines most clearly when you're honest about your weakness.

Weakness doesn't push God away. Weakness invites Him close.

Think about moments from your own season when you felt weak. Maybe you couldn't perform at the level you hoped. Maybe a mistake shook you more than you expected. Maybe you were overwhelmed by school, friendships, or pressure. Maybe you felt invisible on your team. Maybe your confidence dipped for reasons you didn't understand.

In those moments, you may have tried to hide your weakness. You may have tried to look composed or unaffected. Inside, something felt off. You didn't need a motivational speech. You needed grace.

Grace is God's steady kindness toward you. It's His patience, His forgiveness, His help, His presence. Grace doesn't demand perfection. Grace doesn't wait for you to pull yourself together. Grace moves toward you exactly as you are.

God's grace is sufficient, not barely enough, but fully enough.

When your strength runs out, His strength steps in.

When your confidence cracks, His presence steadies you.

When your effort falls short, His love remains unchanged.

When you feel unworthy, His grace reminds you of your worth.

When your heart feels too heavy, His comfort holds you up.

Athletes often measure themselves by results. God measures you by your heart. He knows that some of the deepest growth happens not when you feel strong, but when you finally admit you can't do everything alone.

Paul learned that weakness wasn't something to fear: it was something God could use. Weakness made room for God's power. Weakness softened his heart. Weakness brought him closer to God. Weakness opened the door for deeper faith.

The same can be true for you.

If you stop acting like you're invincible, you give God room to make you stronger. When you stop trying to impress others, you can finally rest. Admitting you don't know everything helps you listen for God's voice. Recognizing your limits lets you see how endless God's love is.

God's power is made "perfect" in weakness, not because weakness is good, but because it reveals how strong God truly is. When you rely on Him, you carry a strength that doesn't crumble under pressure.

Think about a time when you made it through something you didn't think you could handle. Maybe you were nervous, unsure, or discouraged. Yet you made it through anyway. That wasn't luck. That was grace. God was carrying you even if you didn't realize it.

Grace is God helping you take one more step when you want to quit.

Grace is God calming your fears before a big moment.

Grace is God whispering truth when lies fill your mind.

Grace is God giving you peace that doesn't make sense.

Grace is God showing you that your worth doesn't rise and fall with your performance.

Grace transforms how you see yourself.

Instead of seeing weakness as embarrassment, you begin to see it as a place where God meets you with gentleness. Instead of seeing mistakes as identity-shakers, you see them as moments God can shape you. Instead of seeing pressure as your enemy, you see it as a chance to lean on Him more fully.

Some young athletes think relying on God makes them fragile. The opposite is true. Relying on God makes you resilient. You become steady because your strength comes from Someone who never runs out.

Imagine walking into your next game or practice not with pressure swirling in your chest, but with this prayer in your heart: "Lord, Your grace is enough for me today."

Imagine how light your steps would feel.

Imagine how calm your mind would be.

Imagine how free you would feel playing for the God who loves you, not for approval from others.

When grace fills your heart, pressure loses its grip.

When grace supports you, failure doesn't define you.

When grace surrounds you, you can face challenges with quiet courage.

You won't always feel strong, but you don't need to.

God's grace covers the weak places.

God's strength stands in the gaps.

God's presence stays when your own confidence fades.

Let this verse reshape the way you see your strength. You are not failing when you feel weak. You are not falling apart. You are being invited into deeper trust.

Before your next challenge, slow down for a moment and whisper: "Lord, Your grace is enough."

Let those words settle into your heart. Let them lift the pressure off your shoulders. Let them remind you that God's strength is steady even when yours is not.

Weakness is not the end of your story. It's the place where God begins His work.

Chapter 37

"Be kind and compassionate to one another, forgiving each other, just as in Christ God forgave you." - Ephesians 4:32

Every team faces times when your character is tested more than your skills. Maybe someone snaps at you in practice. Sometimes a teammate ignores your encouragement. A friend might let you down. A coach's words might hurt more than you thought they would. Misunderstandings come up, tension rises, and people get frustrated. In those moments, it's easy to react the same way you were treated.

This verse calls you to something better: *"Be kind and compassionate... forgiving each other."*

Kindness is not weakness.

Compassion is not softness.

Forgiveness is not pretending nothing happened.

These are marks of a strong heart: stronger than any physical ability you bring to your sport.

Athletes are trained to be tough. Push harder. Shake things off. Don't show emotion. Toughness in sports should never erase tenderness in character. God cares deeply about how you treat people, especially when the moment is tense, uncomfortable, or disappointing.

Kindness matters most when it isn't easy.

Compassion matters most when the other person doesn't seem to deserve it.

Forgiveness matters most when your pride tells you to hold on to the hurt.

Teams fall apart not because of lack of talent, but because hearts grow cold. Little frustrations build into walls. Harsh words echo longer than they should. Silence replaces connection.

Slowly, without anyone naming it, unity fades.

This verse invites you to become a different kind of teammate.

A teammate with a generous heart.

A teammate who doesn't return negativity with negativity.

A teammate who chooses grace when tensions rise.

A teammate who sees people beyond their mistakes.

Kindness isn't about being overly cheerful. Compassion isn't about fixing everyone's problems. Forgiveness isn't about ignoring boundaries. These qualities show up in small, steady choices: choices that often go unnoticed but always matter.

Think about a moment when someone showed you kindness on a rough day. Maybe they encouraged you after a tough drill. Maybe they sat beside you when you struggled, or they smiled right when you were starting to feel invisible.

It could be they offered simple words that steadied your heart when you really needed it. That moment didn't fix everything, but it changed something inside you.

Kindness has weight.

Compassion has power.

Forgiveness has healing built into it.

This verse also connects kindness and compassion to forgiveness for a reason. Most unkind behavior comes from a wounded place. A teammate who lashes out may be tired, stressed, insecure, or hurting in ways you don't and couldn't possibly know about. A friend who ignores you may be overwhelmed. A coach who snaps may be carrying a weight no one sees.

Compassion looks beyond the moment and remembers that everyone carries something.

That doesn't excuse poor behavior, but it softens your response. It helps you take a breath instead of reacting quickly. It helps you choose patience instead of anger. Compassion says, "I don't know what you're carrying, but I'll show grace anyway."

Forgiveness is often the hardest part of this verse. It doesn't ignore the hurt or pretend that words didn't hurt you. It also doesn't mean acting like the moment didn't matter. Forgiveness lets you loosen your hold on the pain so it doesn't control your heart.

Unforgiveness is a silent burden. It takes away your joy and peace. Even if you look calm, your heart feels tense. You bring it with you to practice, games, and conversations. It uses up energy that could help you grow.

When God invites you to forgive, He isn't saying the wrong didn't matter. He's saying *you matter too much to carry what will harm you if it stays inside.*

God knows forgiveness because He has forgiven you completely. Not halfway. Not reluctantly. Fully.

When Paul writes "just as in Christ God forgave you," he's reminding you of the standard. God's forgiveness didn't come because you earned it. It came because of His love. That same love becomes the fountain from which your forgiveness flows.

You can't forgive in your own strength, not deeply, but you can forgive through God's strength working in you.

If forgiveness feels impossible right now, start by praying,

"Lord, soften my heart. Help me to forgive."

That prayer alone opens the door.

Kindness, compassion, and forgiveness also shape the culture around you. A single athlete who carries these traits can shift the feel of an entire team. Your presence can be calming instead of tense, uplifting instead of draining, steady rather than reactive. God often uses one heart to thaw many others.

This doesn't mean you let people walk all over you. Compassion includes boundaries. Forgiveness includes honesty. Kindness includes truth spoken gently. You don't have to become everyone's emotional caretaker. You simply let God shape your reactions so your heart reflects Him more than the moment reflects your frustration.

Think about Jesus, how He treated people who misunderstood Him, doubted Him, hurt Him, and even betrayed Him. He responded with truth, yes, but also with compassion and patience. If He could forgive in the deepest pain imaginable, then through His strength, you can forgive in the smaller hurts of daily life.

Before your next practice or school day, take a quiet moment to do three things:

First, think of someone who has encouraged you recently, even in a small way. Thank God for them.

Second, think of someone who has frustrated you or hurt your heart. Pray for peace toward them.

Third, ask God for eyes that see people the way He sees them.

These steps may feel simple, but they slowly shape your heart into one that reflects Ephesians 4:32.

Imagine what your team would feel like if everyone lived this verse. Imagine what confidence you would carry knowing that kindness doesn't weaken you. It strengthens you. Imagine the freedom of releasing bitterness instead of holding it. Imagine the peace that comes when compassion replaces frustration.

Imagine how God could use your character to point others toward Him.

Let this verse guide your next reaction.

Let it soften your tone.

Let it steady your heart.

Let it lift the weight you've been carrying.

Be kind.

Be compassionate.

Be forgiving.

Not because the people around you are perfect, but because God's love is.

Chapter 38

"Do everything in love." - 1 Corinthians 16:14

There's a moment in almost every season, sometimes more than one, when emotions run hotter than skill drills or game strategy. Maybe it happens when a teammate cuts you off mid-sentence or rolls their eyes.

Maybe it's during a tough scrimmage when someone shoves you a little too hard. Maybe a friend talks behind your back. Maybe you just woke up tired and everything feels louder than it should.

Whatever the reason, it's surprisingly easy to forget love when frustration steps in.

Yet, this verse isn't complicated and doesn't leave much room for excuses.

"Let all that you do be done in love."

It's short, clear, and almost disarming. Love in everything? Even when the situation feels unfair? Even when someone else started the conflict? Even when you're irritated, embarrassed, or fed up?

Yes. Even then.

Love isn't something you flip on only when people behave well. It's something you choose, especially in the moments when you'd rather not.

The real test of love isn't a peaceful day when everyone is getting along. The test shows up when tensions rise, when nerves feel thin, or when the stakes feel high.

If you think about your team or your school or even your own family, you probably know exactly how fast a single harsh reaction can shift the atmosphere. One sarcastic comment. One groan. One glare. It doesn't take much to darken a moment.

Once it happens, it spreads. The mood changes. People shut down or get defensive. And the whole place starts to feel heavier.

It works the other way too.

One kind word can lift someone who's been dragging all day.

One smile can remind a teammate they're valued.

One quiet "Hey, you good?" can soften frustration.

One small gesture can break through a wall someone spent weeks building.

Sometimes, love is loud, but most of the time love is quiet and subtle and almost unremarkable, except to the person who needed it.

What makes love complicated is that it asks something from you when you'd rather stay comfortable. It asks you to soften instead of react. It asks you to listen instead of assuming. It asks you to forgive instead of replaying the moment again and again.

None of that comes naturally, especially for athletes who spend so much of life in competitive settings.

The verse doesn't say, "Let your pleasant moments be done in love." It says *all* that you do.

Love isn't simply a warm feeling. It's more like a steady frame you build your decisions on. You might not feel loving at all times, but you can act in love anyway. Love shows up in effort, tone, timing, patience, presence, honesty, and sometimes silence.

Love is the way you carry yourself around others, especially when you're not at your best.

There's also another layer here: how you treat yourself. Many young athletes speak to themselves with less kindness than they give strangers. You replay mistakes for hours. You push yourself harder than necessary. You judge your worth by results or playing time. You assume everyone else is doing better than you.

Love, true love from God, doesn't shame or belittle. It doesn't call you names in your head. It doesn't say, "You're only valuable if you perform well." Love is patient with the process. Love allows room to grow.

Love forgives when you mess up. If you won't speak kindly to yourself, eventually it becomes harder to speak kindly to others.

Letting everything you do be done in love has a surprising way of steadying your heart. Love slows you down inside, even if life around you stays hectic. It helps you see the actual person behind the attitude. It helps you take a breath before reacting. It helps you notice who might be hurting. It helps you compete fiercely without losing compassion.

This doesn't mean you pretend everything is fine or avoid speaking the truth. Love can be firm. Love can correct. Love can say, "That wasn't okay," or "We need to handle this better." Love never aims to wound. It aims to restore.

Think for a moment about someone on your team or in your life who seems tough on the outside. Maybe they rarely smile. Maybe they carry themselves like nothing ever gets to them. Usually, there's more behind that exterior than anyone knows. Stress. Fear. Pressure. Insecurity.

They might be the very person who needs kindness the most, even though they'd never say it.

Then, think about the people you find the easiest to love, those teammates or friends who make the day brighter without trying. You don't have to force love with them. It just comes naturally.

The verse isn't calling you to love only those who are easy. It reaches into the places where bitterness or frustration sits. That's where love shows its strength.

People will not always treat you well. They will misunderstand you, disappoint you, or offend you. You will do the same at times, because you're human too.

Love doesn't ignore hurt, but it doesn't let hurt rule your heart either.

The more you walk with God, the more you begin to understand that love is not something you produce on your own. It begins with Him. You love because Christ loves you. You forgive because He forgave you first.

You show patience because He has shown you patience so many times. When you realize how deeply and consistently God loves you, it becomes a lot easier to pour that love out.

Before your next game or practice or even class, take a second and whisper: "Lord, let what I do today be done in love."

Not perfection. Not pressure. Not pride. Just love.

Let it guide your reactions.

Let it soften your edges.

Let it steady your tone.

Let it shape the way you compete and the way you treat people.

Love leaves a mark far beyond wins and losses. It influences hearts long after the season ends. It reveals Christ more clearly than any speech or highlight reel ever could.

Let everything you do be done in love, because love is the strongest thing you carry.

Chapter 39

"And over all these virtues put on love, which binds them all together in perfect unity." - Colossians 3:14

There's something familiar about getting dressed for practice or a game. You know the routine: shoes, socks, jersey, warm-ups, and any gear your sport requires. Some days you rush, other days you move slowly, but you never step on the field or court without what you need.

Paul uses that same idea when he says to "clothe yourselves with love." It's a picture that makes sense: love isn't just a feeling, and it isn't something you wait around for. It's something you *put on*, intentionally, the same way you slip into your uniform. You choose it before the day begins. You choose it again when the day gets messy. You choose it when emotions rise and when patience slips.

Love becomes something you wear, not just something you feel.

In the verses before this one, Paul lists several traits that shape how you treat people: compassion, gentleness, patience, and humility. Each of these matters, but none of them can hold together unless love is present. It's like building a team with talented players but no unity. Everything looks good on paper, but it falls apart when the pressure hits.

Love is the glue.

Love keeps things steady when tension rises.

Love makes all the other virtues work.

In sports, you see this clearly. A team might have gifted athletes, but if they don't play for each other, the whole thing feels unstable. One bad moment can spark conflict. One harsh word can shift the mood. One selfish action can unravel trust.

When trust breaks, even simple plays become difficult, but when a team is united. When love shapes the way they treat each other, everything feels different. People listen. They forgive faster. They support one another. They fix issues before they grow. The environment becomes safer, lighter, and more enjoyable. Love creates room for growth, even on rough days.

This verse invites you to carry that kind of love, steady, intentional, active, into every part of your life, not just your sport.

What does it mean to "clothe" yourself in love?

It means starting your day with a decision: "Today, I'm choosing love, whatever comes."

It means reminding your heart that love must lead you, even when emotions swirl.

It means asking yourself: *How would love act in this moment?*

How would love speak?

How would love respond?

Not because you feel like it, but because you follow Christ.

Love is something you wear even when you're tired.

Even when you're annoyed.

Even when you feel wronged.

Even when the situation feels unfair.

Some days, wearing love will feel easy. Other days, it will feel like slipping into gear that's two sizes too small.

That's normal.

Love gets tested in real places:

The moment a teammate snaps at you.

The moment someone spreads a rumor.

The moment your coach corrects you sharply.

The moment a friend pulls away.

The moment jealousy rises.

The moment you feel ignored or disrespected.

In those moments, love isn't a warm feeling. It's a choice.

Sometimes, love looks like patience you didn't think you had.

Sometimes, love looks like a quiet apology.

Sometimes, love looks like giving someone space.

Sometimes, love looks like a second chance.

Sometimes, love looks like refusing to talk badly behind someone's back.

Sometimes, love looks like speaking truth gently.

Sometimes, love looks like staying calm when everything in you wants to fire back.

Wearing love changes how you see people too. It reminds you that each person on your team< each friend, each classmate, each coach, is a whole human with their own battles, fears, hopes, and stress. Love helps you see beyond behavior and into the heart. It reminds you that everyone has rough edges, including you.

There will be days when you don't wear love well. It could be when you lose patience, feel offended, mutter something under your breath, or react before thinking. God doesn't abandon you in those moments. He always invites you to try again, to "put love back on," even if you slipped out of it for a minute.

What makes this verse even more powerful is the phrase "above all."

Above talent.

Above discipline.

Above toughness.

Above skill.

Above results.

Above effort.

Love comes first.

Talent may open doors, but love builds relationships. Discipline may push you forward, but love keeps your heart steady. Toughness may help you face conflict, but love helps you handle it well.

When love leads, everything else gains clarity.

Think about someone you admire for their character. Chances are, love has something to do with it. Maybe they treat people well and they lift others up. Maybe they bring calmness to tense moments, or speak with kindness. Maybe they listen when others don't. Those qualities aren't accidents. They come from a heart ruled by love.

Real love, the kind God grows in you, takes courage. It means choosing unity when division feels easier. It means being steady when others stir drama. It means forgiving even when you have reasons not to. It means caring about the person more than the argument.

Before your next practice or game, take a simple moment and pray, "Lord, help me put on love today."

You don't need the perfect words.

You don't need a long speech.

You just need willingness.

As you step onto the field or court, imagine love as part of your uniform, something that moves with you, shapes your tone, guides your reactions, and softens your approach.

You'll be surprised at how different your day feels when love leads the way. People respond differently. Tension fades faster. You feel lighter inside. The team feels more connected. And your own heart grows stronger.

Let love be the thing you carry above everything else.

Let love be what holds your team together.

Let love be what shapes your words and choices.

Let love reflect Christ in you.

Because when all that you do is done in love, you become a light, steady, gentle, unmistakable, in every place God has put you.

Chapter 40

"Therefore *encourage one another and build each other up, just as in fact you are doing.*" - *1 Thessalonians 5:11*

Team environments have a way of shifting that outsiders might not notice. One day, everyone feels close, but the next, there's a sense of distance. Sometimes practice is easy and fun, but the next time, it feels heavy for reasons you can't explain.

Maybe the drills were tough that day. Maybe someone lost their temper at the wrong time. Or maybe people brought worries from home or school into the gym without realizing it.

In the middle of all this, Paul gives a simple instruction: *"Encourage one another and build each other up."*

It sounds small, almost too obvious, but the longer you play sports, or honestly, live life, you realize how rare and needed encouragement really is.

Think about a moment when somebody encouraged you on a day you weren't doing well. Maybe it was a teammate who said, "Keep going, you're alright." Or a coach who noticed your effort even when the result wasn't great.

Maybe it was a friend who sat next to you when you were quiet and didn't force you to talk. It's strange how such a small act can steady you more than you expect.

Encouragement works like a hand on your back, not pushing you, just reminding you that you're not as alone as you feel.

Paul goes even further, saying, "build each other up." That's different from cheering someone on during warm-ups or shouting their name after a good play. Building someone up is slower. It's quieter. It takes a little more heart. It looks like noticing the teammate who's shutting down after mistakes.

It looks like giving credit instead of trying to claim it. It looks like staying patient when someone is having a rough day without making them feel worse.

Some of the strongest athletes are the ones who keep their eyes open, not just for the ball or the clock, but for the people around them.

There's a lot you don't see in others. A teammate might look fine and still feel discouraged. Someone who jokes a lot might be hiding something heavy. Someone who's unusually frustrated might feel embarrassed about how they're playing.

People tend to bury what hurts them. Encouragement helps pull them back to steady ground.

Encouragement is also one of the quickest ways to shift the mood of an entire team. One kind sentence can shake loose the tension that built up all practice. One sincere compliment can loosen the knot in someone's chest. It doesn't fix everything, of course, but it makes things lighter.

Sometimes lightness is enough for that day.

Encouragement doesn't always come naturally. Some days, you're tired of your own problems. Some days, you feel overlooked or frustrated, and the idea of lifting someone else feels unfair.

Oddly enough, those are the days when encouraging someone else often helps you too. It doesn't magically erase your pressures, but it opens a window in your heart that lets a little warmth back in.

Encouragement isn't pretending everything is perfect. It's noticing what is still good. It's saying, "I see you trying."

It's saying, "You matter to this team."

It's saying, "Don't give up on yourself yet."

It's also saying things you don't always feel brave enough to say, like:

"I'm sorry."

"I was too harsh earlier."

Or, "Are you doing okay? You seemed off today."

Building someone up sometimes means being honest with them too, but with a tone that helps instead of harms. You can correct someone while still showing them that you believe in their potential.

Paul ends the verse by saying, "just as in fact you are doing." I like that part. It's almost as if he's saying, "You're on the right track, just keep going." It's a reminder that encouragement shouldn't be a special occasion. It should be a habit, a pattern you return to again and again.

You don't need to be the most outgoing person on your team to encourage others. Quiet people often encourage the best because they do it without expecting attention. You don't need speeches. You don't need to force it. Encouragement lands best when it sounds like you.

A few words in the hallway.

A quick pat on the back.

A moment of eye contact that says, "You've got this."

A small smile from across the room when someone is spiraling inside their head.

These tiny things matter more than you think.

Before your next practice or school day, ask God to show you one person who needs encouragement. He'll bring someone to mind. It might surprise you who it is. Sometimes the person who looks the strongest is carrying the most weight.

You don't have to fix their situation. You don't have to have the perfect words. You just have to be willing to show up for them.

Encouragement is one of the clearest ways the love of Christ shines through you. People may forget big speeches or fancy phrases, but they remember who stood beside them. They remember who helped them breathe again. They remember who lifted them when they felt small.

Encourage one another.

Build each other up.

It may feel small, but it echoes longer than you know.

PART V
Faith Set, Team Set:
Trusting God & Serving Others

Chapter 41

"Do not let any unwholesome talk come out of your mouths, but only what is helpful for building others up according to their needs, that it may benefit those who listen.." - Ephesians 4:29

Words seem small... until they land in the wrong moment.

A quick joke that cuts deeper than you intended.

A frustrated comment said under your breath.

A teammate's mistake that hits your patience the wrong way.

A coach's direction that sparks irritation.

A friend's bad day that collides with your own frustration.

Young athletes talk a lot every day, on the field, in group chats, during warm-ups, after school, on the bus, in the locker room. Because of that, it becomes easy to forget how much strength or harm a single sentence can hold.

Ephesians 4:29 speaks with a steady kind of clarity.

It says your words should build, always building, not tearing down. That means your voice is not only a sound. It's a tool. And God cares about how you use it.

Athletes deal with intense moments, missed plays, loud mistakes, tired bodies, mixed emotions, and competitive edges that scrape against each other during hard practices. In those moments, words can fly out before you even think.

This verse calls you to slow your reactions and consider the effect your voice has on the people around you.

Your words are part of your character. They reveal what's happening inside you. They show whether you're ruled by frustration or guided by love.

Here's something important: You don't have to shout to hurt someone. Quiet negativity can do it too. Sarcasm can do it. Rolling your eyes can do it. A dismissive tone can do it. A careless sentence said in a moment of irritation can stay with someone longer than you ever realize.

The opposite is true as well. A calm word can lift someone's spirit. A simple "You've got this" can settle nerves. A gentle correction can help a teammate grow. A kind sentence at the right moment can change someone's whole day.

"Only what is helpful for building others up."

Think of a construction site. Construction takes time, effort, patience, and intention. Demolition takes only a few seconds. Many people use words like demolition tools, quick, loud, damaging, but God calls you to be the builder.

Being a builder with your words doesn't mean pretending everything is perfect. It doesn't mean ignoring mistakes. It means valuing people more than your frustration. It means speaking in a way that reflects Christ, even when the moment tempts you to react instead of respond.

Picture a teammate who just messed up a drill for the third time. You can react with annoyance, or you can respond with something steady.

Picture yourself making a mistake and feeling embarrassed. Wouldn't you want someone to encourage you instead of pointing out your failure?

That's why words matter. They shape the environment you're part of.

Teams with encouraging voices are stronger.

Teams with harsh voices crumble in quiet ways long before a scoreboard says anything.

Your words also shape *you*.

If your mouth becomes a place where frustration spills out, your heart grows used to irritation.

If your mouth becomes a place where kindness lives, your heart becomes more patient, more grounded, more like Christ.

Some young athletes use harsh words because they think it makes them tough. True toughness is choosing the harder thing: steady speech when emotions rise. Kindness when tempers flare. Calm words when the room is loud. Anyone can say something sharp. Strength is found in saying something that heals.

Ephesians 4:29 doesn't ask you to speak perfectly. It asks you to speak purposefully. Before a sentence leaves your mouth, it invites you to ask one simple question: "Does this build or does this break?"

Think about how different your practices and games could feel if everyone on your team asked that one question before speaking. Think about the peace that would settle over your environment. Think about the trust that would form. Think about the confidence that would grow, not just in you, but in the people beside you.

Here's something many athletes forget: building others up builds you too.

When you speak with life, your heart softens.

When you speak encouragement, your purpose sharpens.

When you speak with kindness, your confidence grows because you know you're acting in a way that honors God.

You don't need a loud personality to build up others. Quiet voices can encourage just as powerfully. You don't need the spotlight. You don't need a starting position. You don't need perfect social skills. You only need a willing heart and the courage to speak in a way that reflects Christ.

This verse also challenges the words you speak inside your own head. Sometimes the harshest comments aren't spoken out loud, they're whispered to yourself. Words like "I'm not good enough," "I always mess up," or "I'll never improve." Those don't build anything. They break your spirit. And they don't come from God.

God's voice builds.

Shame destroys.

Learn to recognize the difference.

So, how do you practice this verse as an athlete? Not through long speeches, but through small choices: a steady tone, a gentle correction, a sincere compliment, a calm breath before speaking, a simple "Good job," a quiet prayer before reacting, a willingness to hold your tongue when frustration flares.

Every kind word becomes a brick that helps build trust.

Every gentle answer becomes a plank that supports unity.

Every encouraging sentence becomes a beam that strengthens your team.

Building takes time. Breaking takes a moment. Choose the path that honors God.

Before you step onto the field or court this week, take a few seconds to pray: "Lord, guide my words today. Help me speak in a way that builds."

Let your voice carry strength rooted in love, not anger.

Let your words be a place where people feel steady, not small.

Let your speech reveal the work God is doing inside you. Your words are powerful. Use them to build.

Chapter 42

"Do not let your hearts be troubled. You believe in God; believe also in Me." -John 14:1

There are days when your heart feels unsettled, even if you can't point to one exact reason. Maybe you're nervous about getting playing-time. Maybe school is piling up or friendships feel off. Maybe you're just "tired" in a way sleep doesn't seem to fix.

A troubled heart doesn't always show itself on the outside. Sometimes you smile, you go to practice, you joke around, but inside something keeps tightening.

Jesus spoke this verse to His disciples during a moment when things felt uncertain for them. Their future looked unclear. Change was coming. Fear was coming. Jesus didn't ignore any of that. He didn't pretend their worries were silly. He simply told them the one thing their hearts needed most:

"Do not let your hearts be troubled."

Not because the world was calm.

Not because everything made sense.

Not because the next days would be easy, but because **He** was with them.

For young athletes, this hits close to home. You're expected to stay composed through pressure, decisions you can't control, and quiet fears that build inside your chest. You hear phrases like "shake it off," "don't think about it," or "just get over it."

Jesus doesn't speak to you like that. He speaks straight to the heart, the part of you that gets tight, overwhelmed, or anxious.

A troubled heart feels like running while carrying a backpack full of weights. You can still move, but everything takes more effort. You try to focus, but stress keeps bumping into your attention. You try to enjoy your sport, but pressure wraps around your thoughts.

Jesus doesn't ask you to pretend the weight isn't there. He asks you to let Him carry it.

"Believe in God; believe also in Me."

This is not just belief in the sense of "agreeing with something." It's trust. Real trust. The kind that lets your shoulders drop because you know Someone bigger is holding the world you're worried about.

A troubled heart usually comes from three places:

The fear of what might happen.

The pressure of what's happening right now.

The weight of something that already happened.

Jesus speaks gently into all three.

He tells you that the future doesn't have to scare you when He is guiding it.

He tells you that the present doesn't have to crush you when He is near.

He tells you that the past doesn't define you when He forgives and restores.

When He says, "Do not let your hearts be troubled," He isn't giving a rule to follow. He's offering rest.

Think about a time when you were anxious and someone you trusted simply sat with you. They didn't fix everything. They didn't try to sound wise. They were just there. Their presence steadied you. You could breathe again.

Jesus offers that kind of presence, but stronger: present in every moment, not limited by distance or time.

Sometimes, a troubled heart shows up in sports more than anywhere else. You try to hide it in warm-ups or under a tough expression, but it reveals itself in small ways: tight shoulders, shallow breaths, hesitation, frustration that grows faster than it should. You might even wonder why you feel this way when nothing "big" happened.

Your heart doesn't need something dramatic to feel troubled. Pressure alone can stir it up.

Jesus knows this. He isn't asking you to fight your anxiety alone. He isn't asking you to be tougher or more stoic. He's inviting you to trust Him with the part of you that feels fragile.

Maybe you've prayed before and didn't feel an immediate change. That doesn't mean He didn't hear you. Sometimes, peace grows slowly, the way the sun rises, not all at once, but bright enough to chase away the dark.

Trust also grows in small steps.

"I'm worried, but I trust You."

"I don't understand, but I trust You."

"I feel tense, but I trust You."

These are honest prayers. Jesus receives them.

Do not underestimate what it means to bring your troubled heart to Him. Athletes are often taught to hide weakness, but a troubled heart is not a weakness. It's a sign you need the Father's comfort. Scripture never shames you for that. Jesus' words here prove it.

Believing in Jesus is not about ignoring your emotions. It's about letting Him guide your emotions instead of letting fear guide them. When your heart begins to race, you can pause, even in the middle of practice, and pray quietly,

"Lord, calm my heart."

It doesn't have to be fancy. God hears short prayers too.

Peace rarely enters loudly. It usually arrives through steady reminders:

You are held.

You are loved.

Your future is in God's hands.

Your worth isn't based on performance.

You're allowed to breathe.

You're allowed to rest.

You're allowed to let Him carry what you cannot.

This verse also invites you to trust that Jesus sees what you can't see. When you don't know what's coming next, He does. When you feel like everything is shifting, He stays steady. When you wonder if you'll make it through a tough season, emotionally, spiritually, or physically, He whispers that He's already there in the places you fear.

A troubled heart often comes from feeling alone in your stress. Jesus begins by reminding you that you never are.

Before your next game, test, practice, or conversation, pause for just a moment and breathe slowly. Say quietly, "Lord, settle my heart."

Let that be your starting point.

His peace doesn't depend on your circumstances.

His peace doesn't depend on how well your day goes.

His peace doesn't depend on your strength.

His peace depends on Him, and He doesn't change.

You may still face challenges. You may still feel nervous. You may still have days that stretch you, but you don't walk into any of those moments alone. Jesus' voice goes with you:

"Do not let your hearts be troubled." Not because the path is easy, but because He walks it with you. That truth, steady and simple, is enough to bring peace to even the most overwhelmed heart.

Chapter 43

"There is no fear in love. But perfect love drives out fear, because fear has to do with punishment. The one who fears is not made perfect in love." -1 John 4:18

Fear looks different for every athlete. Sometimes it's loud, and hits your stomach before a big game. Sometimes it's quiet and whispers when you lie in bed at night thinking about mistakes you made or moments you wish you handled better.

Sometimes, it shows up as pressure, or second-guessing, or worrying about what other people think. Fear doesn't always feel like fear. It often hides underneath thoughts you've gotten used to carrying.

John writes something bold: *"Perfect love casts out fear."*

Not "helps you manage fear."

Not "reduces fear a little."

Cast out, like throwing something heavy off of you so you can finally breathe.

Fear doesn't disappear because you get stronger, or perform better, or impress people. Fear loses its grip when love takes its place.

And not just any love: God's love. Steady love. Deep love. Love that doesn't move when your confidence does.

Fear feeds off the idea that you aren't enough. God's love answers that before the question even forms: *You are Mine. You are loved. I am with you.*

Fear depends on the thought that you have to earn your worth. God's love settles the truth: *Your worth was decided long before you ever held a ball or put on a jersey.*

Fear tells you that your future is uncertain. God's love reminds you that He holds your future with care.

Some young athletes don't realize how much fear shows up in their sport. It hides inside hesitations, hesitating to take a shot, to speak up, to fail in front of others. It hides inside comparison, feeling like everyone around you is doing better, moving faster, improving more quickly.

It hides inside pressure: believing every mistake proves something about who you are.

Fear tries to shape your view of yourself. God's love reshapes it back.

When you feel fear rise in your chest, it usually comes with a handful of questions:

"What if I fail?"

"What if people think less of me?"

"What if I'm not enough?"

"What if I never get this right?"

God's love answers each question, not with a lecture, but with presence. His love isn't distant. It meets you where fear usually forms: in your mind, in your thoughts, in the quiet places you don't talk about.

Perfect love doesn't mean you will never feel nervous or unsure. Perfect love means fear doesn't get to lead. Fear may show up, but it doesn't get to decide your steps. Love does.

Think about someone in your life who makes you feel safe, someone you can be honest with without pretending. Around them, your shoulders drop. Your breath slows. You don't worry about earning their approval. That safety comes from love.

Now stretch that feeling out wider and deeper. That's how God holds you.

He isn't waiting for you to have perfect games or perfect days. He carries you the same on a rough night as He does on a great one. His love is not measured by your stats, your progress, or the role you're given on your team. His love is grounded in who He is, not what you accomplish.

When you step onto a field or court with a heart full of fear, everything feels heavier. Your movements tighten. Your thinking gets cloudy. You play small. You hesitate. You overthink the simplest decisions. Fear shrinks you inside before you even take your first step.

When you step into the same moment with a heart rooted in God's love, something shifts. You play freer. You take healthy risks. You recover from mistakes faster. You stop worrying about who's watching. You let go of the pressure to be perfect.

Love creates room to grow.

Many athletes pray for confidence, but confidence grows best where fear cannot rule. And fear can't rule where love lives. God's love isn't sentimental or soft. It's strong. Strong enough to break through lies you've believed about yourself. Strong enough to lift the pressure you've been carrying. Strong enough to pull fear out at its root.

Here's something important: you have to let the love in. Fear fills whatever space love leaves empty. It speaks louder when you stop reminding yourself of who God is and who you are in Him. Making space for love means slowing down long enough to remember the truth.

Truth like:

God sees me.

God cares about me.

God is not disappointed in me.

God walks into every hard moment with me.

God's love is steady even when I feel shaky.

Fear hates truth. It weakens when truth is spoken over it.

One of the clearest signs that love is growing in you is this: you start talking to yourself with more patience. You stop tearing yourself down after mistakes. You stop telling yourself you're behind, or not enough, or unwanted.

You talk to yourself the way God talks to you: with kindness, honesty, and hope. With love instead of pressure.

Perfect love also influences how you treat others. When your heart is rooted in love, you're less threatened by other people's success. You're less jealous. You're less reactive. You become someone who lifts instead of competes for attention. Love frees you from the need to be the best in order to feel valued.

Fear makes you closed.

Love opens you.

Fear makes you tight.

Love makes you steady.

Fear makes you hide.

Love brings you into the light.

Before your next practice or game, try this simple prayer:

"Lord, fill me with Your love so fear has no place to stay."

Say it slowly. Let it settle. Let it remind you that you walk into every moment with Someone who is not afraid of anything, not even the things that scare you.

God's love isn't fragile. It isn't temporary. It isn't dependent on your mood or your performance. It stands firm even when you don't. When you let that love take root, fear loses its grip.

Perfect love casts out fear, not gently, not gradually, *casts it out.*

Throws it off.

Breaks its hold.

Replaces it with peace that doesn't make sense on paper but feels real in your chest.

Walk into today with love as your anchor.

Let fear fall quiet.

Let love lead.

Because the One who loves you perfectly walks beside you, and with Him, fear doesn't get the final word.

Chapter 44

"Set your mind on things above, not on things on the earth." - Colossians 3:2

There's a moment in almost every season, usually right in the middle, when your thoughts get louder than your actual sport. You're running drills, but your mind drifts. You're doing homework, but you're replaying yesterday's mistakes. You try to sleep, but your brain won't let go of what you fear might happen next game.

You think about who's watching, who's judging, what your coach might be thinking, what your friends might be saying. Your body is present, but your mind has been pulled in a dozen directions.

Paul's instruction in Colossians speaks directly into that mental tug-of-war: *"Set your minds on things above, not on earthly things."*

Set your mind.

Place it somewhere on purpose.

Aim it toward something higher than your stress or your expectations.

Most athletes don't realize how much of their struggle lives in their thoughts. Legs get tired, yes. Arms get sore, of course, but your thoughts often carry the real weight.

And when your mind gets tangled, everything else follows.

Paul isn't telling you to ignore life. He's not saying your sport doesn't matter. He's reminding you that your mind needs an anchor stronger than your emotions, stronger than your pressure, stronger than whatever went wrong today.

"Things above" doesn't mean some imaginary cloud far away. It means what is true, steady, eternal: God's character, God's promises, God's love, God's presence. These are the things that steady you when the world around you (and inside you) feels scattered.

You've probably noticed this: when your thoughts spiral, your performance often dips. Your confidence shrinks. You start playing tight. You rush. You hesitate. You overthink basic decisions.

Sometimes you don't even enjoy the sport you usually love because your mind is somewhere else, usually in a place filled with fear or pressure.

Fear pulls your thoughts down.

Truth lifts your thoughts up.

Setting your mind "on things above" doesn't happen by accident. It's intentional. Almost like choosing where to look while balancing, eyes up instead of staring at the ground.

Let's think about what "earthly things" might mean for a young athlete. It could be trying to impress people, worrying about mistakes, fearing failure, the need to control every outcome, the pressure to be perfect, or frustration with a role you didn't ask for.

These things are real, but they are not strong enough to guide your heart. When your mind stays stuck on them, they drain you. They distract you. They chip away at your peace.

When you lift your focus, even slightly, by turning your thoughts toward God, everything starts to shift. Not instantly, not magically, but gradually. You remember who He is. You remember who you belong to. You remember that your worth doesn't rise and fall with a good day or a bad one.

Setting your mind "on things above" means remembering:

"God is with me."

"God loves me."

"God sees the whole picture."

"God steadies my steps even when I feel shaky."

"God holds my future."

"God's truth matters more than my fears."

When these thoughts take root, fear loses some of its grip. Pressure loosens. The tightness in your chest starts to ease. You can breathe again.

Think about how a coach might redirect you during a drill. "Head up." "Stay centered." "Look forward." The instructions sound simple, but they change everything about how your body moves.

God's instruction here is similar: *Lift your thoughts. Steady your attention. Look higher.*

Your mind is powerful. What you focus on shapes how you feel, the choices you make, your confidence, and even your habits. Paul sees your thought life as something important, not just a small detail. It's at the center.

Let's be honest. It's hard to focus on higher things when your heart feels messy. On tough days, your thoughts can fall apart fast. You might try to focus on God, but your mind wanders again in seconds. That's not failure. It just means you need more practice.

You train your body with reps, drills, and repetition. You train your mind the same way.

It might look like:

Opening Scripture for five quiet minutes before school.

Breathing deeply before a game and whispering, "Lord, steady my mind."

Replacing a negative thought with a truth from God.

Pausing mentally when frustration rises.

Remembering you are loved, even when you feel overwhelmed.

Choosing not to let someone else's comment define your mood.

Small things, repeated consistently, shape your thinking.

You don't need to become an expert at controlling your thoughts. You need to learn how to redirect them. There's a difference. Controlling is about forcing. Redirecting is about gently lifting your focus back where it belongs.

God never meant for you to carry the weight of every fear alone. He invites you to lift your eyes, not because He wants to ignore your life, but because He wants to help you see it clearly.

When your mind is set on things above, you move differently. You become steadier. People's opinions lose some of their control. Pressure doesn't crush you as easily. You can play with freedom, not fear. You can grow without constantly worrying about messing up.

Strangely, lifting your thoughts toward God often helps you stay more grounded in real life, because your confidence starts coming from a deeper place. Not from approval. Not from performance, but from Someone who does not change.

Before your next practice or game, try this: Place your hand over your heart for a moment. Breathe slowly.

Pray quietly: "Lord, help me set my mind on things above."

Not long.

Not complicated.

Just honest.

Say it again in the middle of a drill if you feel overwhelmed. Say it when you feel comparison creeping in. Say it when your thoughts start spiraling into negativity. Each time you say it, you're lifting your focus a little higher.

Your sport matters. Your goals matter. Your feelings matter. But they don't make a good foundation for your mind. God does.

Let your thoughts rise.

Let your heart settle.

Let your mind rest in the truth of who He is.

Because when your thoughts have a higher place to land, your whole life follows.

Chapter 45

"Trust in the Lord with all your heart and lean not on your own understanding." - Proverbs 3:5

There are stretches in every athlete's life when nothing seems to line up the way you expected. You train hard, but the results don't show. A coach's decision stings more than you want to admit. A teammate moves ahead of you. An injury slows you down.

Or maybe the stress isn't from your sport at all, maybe something outside of it is tugging at your attention and leaving you worn out. You keep trying to figure everything out, replaying details in your head until you feel even more confused than when you started.

This verse lands right in the center of that frustration. *"Trust in the Lord with all your heart..."*

Not half your heart. Not the portion left over after stress eats the rest. All of it.

It's a simple sentence, but one that feels heavier when life doesn't make sense. Trust is easy when things go the way you imagined.

Trust feels manageable when progress is visible, but when doors close, or timing feels wrong, or confusion grows louder than clarity, trust becomes something deeper. Something you choose before you know the outcome.

Most young athletes try to understand everything on their own. You look for signs. You overthink. You replay conversations. You wonder why something happened and how long it'll take for things to change.

Your mind works overtime trying to solve problems that refuse to line up. The more you lean on your own understanding, the more exhausted you feel.

Understanding has limits. Trust does not.

When God says, "lean not on your own understanding," He isn't asking you to shut off your brain. He's inviting you to loosen your grip. Your mind can analyze, but it cannot control the path. It cannot predict every step. It cannot guarantee outcomes.

When you try too hard to understand everything, it can leave you feeling frustrated. Some things are simply meant for God to handle, not us.

Trust is about believing that God sees things you can't. He knows what's coming, and He understands the strengths He is building in you.

He knows what needs to shift inside your heart long before you do, and He knows exactly why the path bends when you hoped it would stay straight.

Remember a time when life felt uncertain, whether it was earlier this year or even now. It may have been stressful, but looking back, you can probably see how much you learned. You might also realize that what you wanted then wasn't actually the best for you.

Perhaps you still don't understand, but you can sense that God carried you through. Trust rarely comes from understanding. Often, understanding comes later, after trust has already done its work.

Athletes often like to feel in control of their routines, their performance, their improvement, their role on a team.

So much of your journey sits outside your control. You can work hard, you can prepare well, you can train with focus, and those things matter. The deeper movements in your life, timing, growth, opportunity, healing, belong to God. He isn't careless with them. He isn't late. He isn't confused.

Trust asks you to believe that God is doing something meaningful even when you can't trace the outline of it.

There's a quiet beauty in trusting God with your whole heart. It doesn't look dramatic from the outside. No one else might even notice. It often happens in small inner moments, when you choose to breathe instead of panic; when you pray instead of spiraling; when you decide to stay steady even though your circumstances feel shaky.

Trust settles your heart in ways understanding never can, but trust does not mean pretending you're fine. It does not mean forcing yourself to feel peaceful. It means bringing your real questions and real fears to God and resting them in His hands.

There's no pressure to sound polished. You can say, "God, I don't understand what You're doing, but I'm choosing to trust You anyway." That is trust in its truest form, not coming from certainty, but from surrender.

Sometimes trust feels like recognizing that a closed door is not the end. Sometimes it feels like staying patient when your speed or strength isn't improving as quickly as you hoped. Sometimes it feels like forgiving yourself for mistakes you've carried far too long. Sometimes it feels like giving God the worry that's been sitting in your stomach for weeks.

Sometimes it feels like taking one step forward, even when you're not sure where the next one will land.

When an athlete learns to trust God, something changes in the way they carry themselves. Their shoulders loosen. Their confidence becomes steadier because it isn't tied to daily ups and downs. They bounce back quicker. They play with more freedom.

They stop measuring their worth by performance. They understand that even if life feels uncertain, they are held by Someone who is not uncertain at all.

Trust also has a way of opening your eyes to things you would've missed otherwise. You start noticing small blessings, conversations that encourage you, teammates who support you, moments of progress that once felt too minor to appreciate. Trust shifts your focus from what's missing to what God is quietly providing.

There will be moments when trust feels thin, when you feel yourself slipping back into worry. That doesn't mean you've failed. Trust is not a one-time decision. It's a rhythm. Some days it feels strong; other days you have to rebuild it from scratch. God is patient with both days.

Before your next practice, game, or school day, take a quiet moment and breathe slowly. Let your shoulders relax. Pray something simple and honest, something like: "Lord, help me trust You with all my heart today."

Don't trust in your talent. Don't trust in your understanding. Trust in Him.

You may not know exactly where the path leads. You may not understand why things are unfolding the way they are, but you can trust the One who sees the full picture, Who loves you deeply, and Who has never lost track of you.

Lean on Him. Let your heart rest. Let trust carry you where understanding cannot.

Chapter 46

"Fear not, for I am with you; Be not dismayed, for I am your God. I will strengthen you, Yes, I will help you, I will uphold you with My righteous right hand." - Isaiah 41:10

There are days when strength feels far away. You can wake up tired before the day even begins. You can walk into practice already worn out from school, from friendships, from the pressure you carry quietly.

Some days you push through drills and wonder why everything feels heavier than usual. On other days, you try to stay focused, but your mind feels scattered. You want to be strong, but something inside you keeps slipping.

When God speaks these words, *"I will strengthen you and help you"*, He isn't talking to perfect people. He's speaking to people who feel stretched thin, overwhelmed, unsure, or scared.

He isn't waiting for you to toughen up first. He isn't asking you to hold it together so He can step in afterward. He is offering strength right in the middle of whatever is wearing you down.

"Do not fear, for I am with you."

Those words alone change the entire feel of a hard moment. Fear grows strongest in the places where you feel alone, alone in your thoughts, alone in your stress, alone in your emotions.

Even surrounded by teammates or friends, fear can still whisper that no one understands what you're carrying.

God does, and He doesn't watch from far away. He stays close.

Young athletes face a strange mix of pressures. You're expected to grow up quickly, perform under stress, stay confident, handle disappointment, manage emotions, and keep improving, all at the same time.

It's easy to get overwhelmed. It's easy to reach a point where even simple tasks feel like too much. You don't have to say it out loud for God to see it.

That's why He says, *"Do not be dismayed."* Dismay is deeper than fear; it's the feeling that you don't have enough left to keep going. It's exhaustion mixed with discouragement. It's the voice that says, "I can't do this anymore," even though you keep trying.

God doesn't ignore that feeling, and He doesn't respond by telling you to work harder. Instead, He says, *"I will strengthen you."*

His strength doesn't look like a sudden burst of energy or a dramatic surge of confidence. Sometimes it's quieter. It might come as a calmer heartbeat before a game. It might come as a renewed sense of peace that you weren't expecting. It might show up as the courage to take one more step. It might hide in the small breath you take before you begin again.

Strength from God is steady, not noisy. It meets you at the pace you can handle.

He doesn't shame you for needing help. He knows you were never meant to carry everything on your own.

Then, God says something even more personal: *"I will help you."*

Help. Not judging you. Not look down on you. Not demand more from you before He offers support. Help. That word is simple, but it holds a lot of kindness. It means He steps into the places where you feel weak. It means He lifts what feels too heavy.

It means He fights battles you don't even see. It means He holds the pieces you're afraid are slipping.

Sometimes, the help God gives isn't what you expect. You might pray for one thing and receive something different. While you want everything around you to change, God may start by strengthening your heart instead.

While you want answers, God may give you peace first. While you want a situation to end, God may walk you through it slowly, teaching you what you didn't realize you needed.

His help always comes with purpose, even when you don't understand it yet.

Athletes often feel pressure to produce strength from within themselves at all times. You're supposed to be mentally tough, emotionally steady, physically capable, and always ready to compete.

Remember, though: no one, no matter how talented or dedicated, can be strong every day. Human strength reaches a limit. God's strength does not.

He says, *"I am your God."*

Not just the God of the world or the God of the Scriptures: **your** God, personal and present.

That means He cares about your tired days. He cares about the nights when fear shows up for no clear reason. He cares about the heavy thoughts you keep to yourself, and about the pressure you feel before a game. He cares about your confidence, your exhaustion, your stress, your hopes, and the parts of you that ache quietly.

If He didn't care, He wouldn't have said, *"I will strengthen you and help you."*

When you face something difficult, an injury, a setback, a harsh comment, a tough practice, a season of doubt, your first instinct might be to handle it alone. You might try to push through it with willpower. You might try to hide how you feel. You might try to convince yourself you don't need help.

God isn't waiting for the moment you admit weakness. He's already walking beside you, waiting for you to rest in Him instead of fighting through everything alone.

Imagine stepping into your next practice with this quiet truth in your mind: "I don't face this day in my own strength. God strengthens and helps me."

Your breathing shifts.

Your tension loosens.

Your fear loses some of its control.

Your confidence grows, not because you feel strong, but because you aren't facing anything alone.

God's presence changes how you handle pressure. His strength changes how you face challenges.

God's help changes how you carry your burdens.

This verse is not a promise that life will be easy. It's a promise that you will never walk into a hard moment without God beside you. If He is with you, then you are more supported than you realize.

At some point today, maybe even right now, take a slow breath and pray something honest and simple: "Lord, I need Your strength. Please help me."

Not fancy or long. Just real.

He hears you, He moves toward you.

He strengthens and helps, just as He promised.

Chapter 47

"He tends his flock like a shepherd: He gathers the lambs in his arms and carries them close to his heart; he gently leads those that have young." - Isaiah 40:11

There's a kind of tiredness that sleep doesn't fix. It's the tired that comes from carrying worry for too long, or pushing yourself without stopping, or trying to be strong in every situation even when your heart feels unsteady. Young athletes often learn how to push through pain or fatigue, but no one really teaches you what to do when the exhaustion is deeper, when it's your spirit that feels worn out.

Isaiah writes something gentle, almost like a soft blanket placed over a shivering heart: *"He tends his flock like a shepherd: He gathers the lambs in his arms and carries them close to his heart; he gently leads those that have young."*

This is not a picture of a distant God. This is not a picture of someone who waits for you to get your life together before He comes near. This is a picture of tenderness. Of care. Of closeness. Of God paying attention to every step you take, especially the ones that feel heavy.

Athletes spend a lot of time proving themselves, to coaches, to teammates, to parents, to themselves. You want to show you're capable.

You want to show you belong. You want to show you can handle whatever your sport throws at you.

This verse reminds you of something different: God is not asking you to prove anything. He is asking you to let Him carry you.

A shepherd doesn't stand on a hill shouting instructions. He walks with his flock. He keeps his eyes on the ones who lag behind, the ones who limp, the ones who wander, the ones who seem unsure. When a lamb is too tired to keep going, the shepherd doesn't scold it for slowing the group down. He bends down, picks it up, and presses it close to his chest so it feels his heartbeat.

That's the kind of care Isaiah is describing.

Think about the times this year when you felt stretched thin, when practices felt longer than usual, when school piled up, when friends drifted, when confidence flickered, when you wondered if you had anything left to give.

Maybe you tried to push through without saying anything. Maybe you tried to act strong because you thought that was expected of you, or possibly, you didn't want to be the one who needed help.

God never asks you to pretend. A shepherd knows when a sheep is tired without it having to explain anything. God knows your tiredness even when you hide it behind a quiet smile or a determined face.

He carries you close to His heart, not at a distance, not with reluctance, not with frustration. Close. That closeness matters. It means He knows your fear, your hopes, your pressure, your strengths, your weak spots, your dreams.

He knows the moments when you want to quit but don't. He knows the words you wish you could say out loud. He knows the weight you hold in your chest.

He doesn't step away from any of it.

When a shepherd carries a lamb, he doesn't keep it at arm's length. He gathers it against his chest, where it can feel warmth and hear steady breaths. That closeness settles the lamb. Its shaking slows. Its fear fades. Its heart calms.

This is the kind of comfort God offers you: not a quick fix, not a motivational speech, not a demand to toughen up, but the kind of nearness that steadies your soul.

Many athletes believe strength means handling everything alone, but true strength often shows up when you let God carry what you can't. There is no weakness in leaning on Him. In fact, the moments you allow God to carry you may become the moments that shape your faith the most.

Imagine Him lifting the weight you've been holding: your fear of failing, your worry about letting others down, your doubt about your future in your sport. Imagine Him pulling you close, reminding you that you don't have to earn His love, that you don't have to keep up a brave face, that you don't have to push alone.

When God carries you, the pressure changes. You stop moving from fear. You start moving from peace.

Think about what it feels like when someone truly supports you, not with loud words, but with presence. A teammate who sits beside you when you're frustrated. A friend who listens without trying to fix everything. A parent who gives a quiet nod that tells you they're on your side. Those moments matter to you because they make you feel seen.

Now, imagine that at a level deeper than anything you've ever known. That is God's heart toward you.

He tends you.

He watches over you.

He guides you gently.

He carries you when you're too tired to carry yourself.

You are not a burden to Him. You are not "too much." You are not disappointing Him by needing His help. Scripture makes it clear: He delights in caring for His people.

Here's something else: a shepherd doesn't stop carrying the lamb the moment the path gets smooth again. He carries it until the lamb is steady enough to walk with confidence. God does the same. He walks with you long after the storm settles, long after the pressure lifts, long after the season changes.

If this year has left you weary, confused, or unsure of your next steps, if you feel like the weight on your shoulders has grown heavier, then this verse is God's whisper to you: *Let Me carry you.*

You don't have to fight for His attention.

You don't have to convince Him you're worth His care.

You don't have to act stronger than you feel.

You only need to rest in the arms of the One who holds you close to His heart.

Before you end this chapter, take a small moment, place your hand gently over your chest, breathe slowly, and let this truth settle: "God carries me. He holds me close. He knows my steps."

Let that calm you.

Let that steady you.

Let that remind you that your worth is safe in His hands.

You are cared for by the Shepherd who never leaves His flock behind.

You are held by the One who knows your strength and your limits.

You are safe in His arms.

With Him, you will always have what you need for the road ahead.

Chapter 48

"Commit your way to the Lord; trust in him and he will do this." - Psalm 37:5

Every athlete reaches a point where the path ahead starts to feel uncertain. You have goals you care about. Some you've spoken out loud, others you've kept quiet because you're afraid they sound too big. You want direction. You want progress.

You want clarity, but sometimes the way forward feels cloudy, like you're walking down a hallway with the lights turned off.

Your "way" is more than just your sport. It's your entire direction: your decisions, your habits, your plans, your hopes, your disappointments, your next steps. Athletes spend plenty of time planning: routines, workouts, training schedules, game strategies.

Planning is different from committing. You can plan without trust. Commitment requires handing the plan to God and saying, "Lead me. Hold this. Shape it in Your timing, not mine."

Committing your way to the Lord doesn't mean you stop caring. It doesn't mean you sit back and wait for things to magically work out. It means your heart releases its tight grip on outcomes you were never meant to control.

It means you place your journey into God's hands: the God who sees the full story, not just the part you're standing in right now.

Trusting Him is harder than it sounds, though. You want results. You want a direction you can map out. You want to know your hard work is paying off. You want reassurance that the waiting isn't a waste. You want to feel certain about your next step.

Commitment comes before clarity.

Most people wait for God to explain everything before they trust Him. Scripture flips that. God says, "Trust Me first. Then watch Me work."

When you commit your way to the Lord, you're saying, "God, You can guide me better than I can guide myself." That's not easy for an athlete who's used to pushing, striving, driving forward.

It feels strange to loosen your grip when you've spent so much time trying to tighten it, but trust grows where control loosens.

Some young athletes feel pressure to shape their whole future right now: what team they want to make next year, what position they want to earn, what level they hope to reach.

Your story is much bigger than this season, and God is working in ways you can't fully see. He isn't just preparing you for moments of victory. He's shaping your character, your patience, your resilience, your confidence, your humility, and your faith.

When you hand Him your way, He works in the deep places, places discipline alone can't reach.

That's a promise. God doesn't ignore the path you commit to Him. He steps into it.

The way He acts doesn't always look dramatic. Sometimes, He opens a door you weren't expecting. Sometimes, He closes a door you really wanted, only for you to realize later that it protected you. Other times, He shifts your desires, and in others He strengthens your heart for the challenges ahead.

Sometimes, He brings the right people into your life at the right time. Sometimes, He delays something because He knows rushing it would harm you.

His actions are not random. They're wise, timed with purpose, aimed at your good, even when you don't understand them in the moment.

Think about a time when you pushed hard for something, only to see it fall apart. It hurt. It felt confusing, but maybe later you saw how God used that disappointment to guide you somewhere better. Or maybe you're still waiting for that clarity, but even in the waiting, He's shaping you.

Commitment doesn't mean everything turns out the way you imagined. It means you believe God's way is better, even when it takes a direction you didn't expect.

Young athletes often feel that their identity rests on progress, roles, stats, or the approval of coaches. Committing your way to the Lord shifts that weight. It moves your confidence from your performance to His presence. It reminds you that you are guided by Someone who cannot be shaken.

When you commit your way to God, you can breathe deeper. You don't have to micromanage every detail. You don't have to panic about every change. You don't have to fear falling behind. You don't have to compare your path with someone else's.

Your way belongs to Him.

Your future belongs to Him.

Your pace belongs to Him.

Your story belongs to Him.

Because of that, you lack nothing you truly need to move forward.

It also means you can celebrate others more freely. When you're no longer clinging to your path for dear life, you don't feel threatened by someone else's success. You trust that God is writing your story with intention, not as a copy of someone else's.

There will be days when trusting God feels like standing still. Days when it feels like you're watching other people sprint ahead. Days when you wonder if God remembers your dreams.

Before your next practice, or before you go to sleep tonight, take a quiet moment and place your hand over your chest. Breathe slowly. Say something simple and honest: "Lord, I commit my way to You. Lead me."

You're not asking Him to explain everything. You're inviting Him to go first.

You may not know the whole path ahead, but you know Who walks it with you. When He moves, everything falls into place in ways only He could design.

Chapter 49

"In all your ways acknowledge Him, and He will make your paths straight." - Proverbs 3:6

There's a certain pressure athletes feel that doesn't always get talked about. You're expected to know where you're going, or at least pretend you do. Coaches ask about goals. Teammates ask what you're aiming for.

Adults ask about the future as if you already have a map tucked into your back pocket. Even on days when you feel steady, there's still a quiet part of you that wonders whether you're headed in the right direction.

This verse from Proverbs steps into that uncertainty in a calm, almost gentle way: *"In all your ways acknowledge Him, and He will make your paths straight."*

It doesn't say you need to know every step.

It doesn't say you need a flawless plan.

It doesn't say you have to wow the world with confidence.

It says **acknowledge Him**: bring God into everything you do, not just the moments that feel holy or serious, but the everyday ones too.

"In all your ways" includes the whole range of your life: the warm-ups, the late-night homework, the early morning bus rides, the moments before a game when your stomach twists, the days when confidence feels thin, the days when you're trying to figure out friendships, and the days when nothing seems wrong but something still feels heavy.

To acknowledge God means to remember He's there. It means to look up for a moment, mentally, spiritually, and say, "Lord, I want You in this." Not in a dramatic way. Not in a way that draws attention. More like a steady posture of the heart.

Some athletes think acknowledging God means they have to pray long prayers or talk like someone else.

Often, it's as simple as breathing and whispering something true:

"God, be with me."

"Help me stay steady."

"Guide me."

"Show me the next step."

You don't have to impress Him. You just have to turn toward Him.

When you acknowledge God in your ways, something quiet happens inside your heart. You stop carrying everything on your own shoulders. You stop believing the lie that you have to act older than you are or pretend you have everything figured out.

You stop thinking your entire future rises or falls on one game, one season, one decision, one conversation. You remember that God sees the full picture while you see only one frame.

Then comes the promise: *"He will make your paths straight."*

A straight path doesn't mean an easy one. It doesn't mean a fast one. It doesn't mean a predictable one. It means a **clear** one: clear in the sense that God removes the things that would pull you off course.

Sometimes, He straightens the path by correcting your direction. Sometimes, by closing doors you would have walked through too quickly. Sometimes, by bringing the right people into your life at the right time. Sometimes, by teaching you patience when you wanted speed.

A straight path is a guided path.

Many athletes struggle with the idea of letting God guide them. You're surrounded by messages that say you should create your own destiny, control your own narrative, push your own path forward.

While hard work matters, it's not the same as control. Hard work prepares you. God directs you.

Some of the most frustrating moments in your story might end up being the very things God uses to shape you. Maybe it was the season you didn't start, or the injury that slowed you down, or possibly the tryout that didn't go the way you had hoped.

He worked even in the friendships that shifted. None of these ever feel good in the moment.

Consider this, a path doesn't feel straight when you're standing on it. It feels straight when you look back and realize God guided you through every twist and turn.

Acknowledging God also brings peace into decision-making. You don't have to fear getting everything wrong. When your heart is turned toward Him, He has a way of redirecting your steps if they start drifting.

Shepherds do that. They guide, nudge, protect, and correct. God doesn't abandon you the moment you make a small wrong turn. He gently brings you back.

Some days, acknowledging Him looks like pausing for a second before a big moment and saying, "God, steady me."

Other days it looks like thanking Him for something small you would've rushed past.

Some days it looks like admitting your confusion.

Some days it looks like being honest about your frustration.

Most days it looks like quiet trust, nothing flashy, nothing loud, just steady.

There's something freeing about living this way. You don't have to explain everything. You don't have to force the path forward. You don't have to compare your journey with someone else's.

You don't have to panic when plans change. When you acknowledge God in all your ways, you walk with a different kind of confidence, one that doesn't depend on perfection or performance.

It doesn't mean the path won't include challenges. It means the challenges don't have the power to decide who you are or where you end up.

Maybe you're facing a moment right now that feels unclear. Maybe your role on the team shifted. Maybe you feel stuck and you're trying to figure out why motivation comes and goes.

Do you wish certain things would happen faster, or you feel behind for reasons you can't explain?

This verse invites you to breathe, not rush. Acknowledge God in this moment. Let Him hold the pieces that feel scattered, and let Him shape the story you're trying so hard to control.

Before your next practice or your next game, or even before school tomorrow, take a few quiet seconds and say, "Lord, I acknowledge You in this. Show me the way."

You're not handing Him a polished plan. You're handing Him your heart, and God always knows what to do with a heart that turns toward Him.

He will make your paths straight, not because you walked perfectly, but because He loves guiding those who trust Him.

Chapter 50

"He makes me lie down in green pastures, He leads me beside quiet waters." - Psalm 23:2

Athletes are used to movement. You run, jump, lift, sprint, push, chase, compete. Even on your days off, your mind often refuses to rest. You replay mistakes. You think about what needs improvement.

You wish you had done something differently. You worry about tomorrow's workout or next week's game. Your body may be still, but your thoughts run full speed.

That's why this verse feels so gentle, almost surprising: *"He leads me beside quiet waters."*

God doesn't just guide you toward challenges or growth. He guides you toward rest, real rest, the kind your heart needs even more than your legs do.

Rest doesn't come naturally to most young athletes. You're trained to push through tiredness. You're told that slowing down means falling behind.

You learn to ignore the signals your body and mind send when they're carrying too much. Slowly, without even noticing, you become someone who doesn't quite know how to be still.

God knows this about you, and He knows that strength doesn't grow only through pressure. Strength grows through peace, through quiet, through moments when you finally stop striving and let Him care for you.

When David writes about "quiet waters," he isn't describing a peaceful vacation. He's describing a spiritual state, a place inside your heart where the noise doesn't control you anymore. A place where God's presence becomes louder than fear or stress. A place where you can breathe again.

Sheep won't drink from rushing water. It overwhelms them. They get frightened by the motion. They need calm water, still, safe, gentle. So, a shepherd leads them to a place where they can rest without danger.

You are not so different.

There are forces in your life that feel like rushing water: pressure from coaches, expectations from others, the need to perform well, the fear of disappointing people, the desire to prove yourself, the insecurity that creeps in when someone else seems ahead.

These things stir up your spirit. They make your heart feel noisy. They push you into constant motion.

God sees all of this, and He does not respond by telling you to push harder. He leads you to quiet waters.

Here is the part that many people overlook: You have to let Him lead you.

Quiet doesn't happen by accident. Peace doesn't fall into your lap while you scroll or rush or overthink. You choose to slow your pace long enough to hear His voice. You choose to receive the rest He offers.

You choose to trust that you're not losing anything by pausing. You choose to let God settle the chaos in your chest.

Sometimes, quiet waters look like sitting in your room for a few minutes without your phone.

Sometimes, they look like whispering a short prayer before bed.

Sometimes, they look like taking one slow breath before a game instead of letting nerves decide your mood.

Sometimes, they look like admitting to God, "I'm overwhelmed. Please calm my heart."

Quiet waters are not a place. They are God drawing near.

The verse also says, *"He makes me lie down in green pastures."*

Not "asks me."

Not "suggests."

He makes me.

It's firm, but in the softest way. A shepherd knows when a sheep is exhausted, dehydrated, anxious, or restless. The sheep won't lie down on its own, even when it desperately needs to. It needs the shepherd to guide it to safety and stillness.

God does the same with you. He sees your exhaustion before you do. He sees the pressure wearing down your confidence. He sees the way you keep trying to be strong even when you're running on empty.

Sometimes, He steps in by slowing you down. Not to punish you, but to protect you.

There might be moments in your life when things suddenly pause: a canceled practice, an unexpected break, an injury that interrupts your season, a quieter schedule than you planned.

These moments don't always feel like green pastures at first, but often, they are God creating space you didn't know you needed. Space to breathe. Space to heal. Space to listen.

You are not meant to carry yourself without rest. Even Jesus stepped away from crowds, from noise, from expectations. If the Son of God rested, how much more do you need it?

Quiet waters also remind you that God is gentle. He isn't rushed. He isn't frantic. He isn't overwhelmed. He doesn't demand perfection. His care is calm, steady, and patient. When you let Him lead you beside still waters, you step into the gentleness that has always been part of His heart.

There is something else to notice: quiet waters don't remove challenges. They prepare you for them. Athletes who never rest burn out. Athletes who never slow down lose clarity. Athletes who never settle their minds struggle to stay grounded. Quiet waters strengthen you from the inside out.

When your heart is calm, you respond better to pressure.

When your thoughts settle, you see your sport more clearly.

When your spirit rests, your confidence steadies.

When you feel guided, you stop carrying the world on your shoulders.

Quiet is not weakness. Quiet is strength that comes from God.

If you're reading this and feel overwhelmed, or stretched, or confused, take it as a gentle whisper from God saying, "Let Me lead you. Let Me give you rest you haven't been able to find on your own."

Peace is not found by trying harder.

Peace comes from letting Him lead.

Tonight, or before your next practice, take a moment to sit still. Place your hand on your heart. Breathe slowly. Pray something simple: "Lord, lead me beside quiet waters. Settle my spirit."

You don't need fancy words. You don't need long prayers. You simply need to allow God to do what He already desires: to give you rest, to guide you gently, and to calm the waters inside you.

You are not alone.

You are not forgotten.

You are not meant to be endlessly strong on your own.

The Shepherd is near. Let Him lead you to quiet waters.

Chapter 51

"Be still before the Lord and wait patiently for him; do not fret when people succeed *in their ways, when they carry out their wicked schemes." - Psalm 37:7*

Waiting is one of the hardest things an athlete ever learns to do. You train, you push, you sweat, you focus, and you give your best. Sometimes, you see progress quickly. Other times you feel stuck, even though you're working twice as hard.

There are seasons when improvement is steady and obvious ... and seasons when it's slow and almost invisible.

Then, there are moments when everything feels paused, almost like your life is holding its breath.

Psalm 37:7 speaks straight into that tension: *"Be still before the Lord and wait patiently for Him."*

Stillness feels unnatural for athletes. You're used to motion: running plays, moving your feet, adjusting, reacting, staying active. Coaches shout, "Don't stand still!" because in your sport, stillness usually means you're out of position.

In your spiritual life, stillness before God means something entirely different. It's not weakness. It's not laziness. It's not quitting.

Stillness is trust.

To be still before the Lord means to quiet the part of you that tries to force everything forward. It means taking your hands off the things you were never meant to carry alone. It means sitting long enough to notice that God is nearer than your stress wants you to believe.

Stillness doesn't come easy. Your mind runs ahead, worrying about what's next. You wonder if you're improving fast enough. You wonder if the opportunity you want will ever come. You watch others move forward and wonder why you're stuck waiting.

Waiting can feel like failure when you don't understand it.

That's why this verse matters. God doesn't ask you to wait alone. He asks you to wait *before Him*: in His presence, under His care, within His timing. You're not standing in a long line hoping He remembers you. You are standing close to Him while He shapes something you cannot yet see.

When you wait before the Lord, the waiting itself becomes purposeful. He uses it to strengthen your patience, widen your trust, deepen your peace, and prepare your heart for what's coming next.

For athletes, waiting often feels personal. Maybe you hoped for a certain role on your team and didn't get it, or you're recovering from an injury that keeps you from playing the way you want.

Perhaps the goal you've been working toward seems to keep slipping just out of reach. Maybe other people are getting opportunities you long for. Waiting can bring frustration, and frustration often turns into self-doubt.

God whispers something steady into the middle of that frustration: *"Be still... and wait patiently for Me."*

This doesn't mean doing nothing. You still work hard. You still practice. You still grow, but you stop trying to control outcomes that belong to God. You stop measuring your progress by someone else's timeline. You stop telling yourself that you're behind, or forgotten, or invisible.

Stillness is not about halting your movement, it's about halting your panic.

Think about a moment when your coach asked you to pause during a drill. Sometimes, that pause feels strange. Your body wants to keep moving, but the pause is where you gain clarity. It's where you reset your posture. It's where you see the field differently.

Stillness with God works the same way. It opens your eyes. It steadies your thoughts. It reminds you that you're not rushing ahead alone.

Patience, however, can feel uncomfortable. We live in a world where waiting feels like losing. But patience in Scripture isn't passive. It's active trust. It's believing that God is moving even when you don't see evidence yet.

It's the kind of trust that says, "God, I don't know how long this will take, but I know You don't waste my waiting."

Here's something comforting: God isn't bothered by your questions. He isn't frustrated when you grow impatient. He doesn't roll His eyes when you feel discouraged. He simply keeps inviting you back into stillness, back into trust, back into His presence.

Sometimes, waiting is where the most important things grow. Strength doesn't only grow through action. It grows through surrender. It grows through quiet moments where you learn to hear God's voice above the noise of your fear. It grows through days when everything feels slow but you choose to trust anyway.

There will be seasons in your life when God opens doors quickly. And there will be seasons when He asks you to wait longer than you planned. Both are part of His care.

Some of the best athletes you'll ever meet aren't the ones who rose quickly. They're the ones who learned how to wait well. They learned how to let quiet seasons shape them instead of discourage them. They learned how to stay faithful when no one was cheering. They learned how to trust when nothing made sense.

You can learn that too.

Before your next practice or your next big test or even before you fall asleep tonight, give yourself a moment. Not a long moment, just enough to breathe. Sit still for a few seconds. No rushing. No forcing anything forward. In that stillness, pray something simple: "Lord, here I am. Help me wait with trust."

You don't have to sound impressive. You don't have to pretend you're calm if you're not. You just have to bring your real heart into His presence.

Stillness doesn't solve everything instantly, but it shifts the weight. It places your journey back into God's hands, the safest place it can be.

When you wait before Him, peace begins to grow in places fear once lived.

Be still.

Wait patiently.

God is not late.

He is preparing you, shaping you, guiding you, and when the time comes, He will lead you forward with clarity you couldn't have created on your own.

Your job is not to rush the process. Your job is to stay near the One who guides the process.

Be still before the Lord. He's closer than you think.

Chapter 52

"Being confident of this, that he who began a good work in you will carry it on to completion until the day of Christ Jesus.." - Philippians 1:6

There's something steadying about reaching the final devotion in this book. You've spent a year learning, growing, stretching, stumbling, getting back up, and seeing how God meets you in the middle of real life. Some weeks may have encouraged you. Some may have challenged you. Some may have come at the exact moment you needed them. And now you're arriving at a verse that feels like a hand on your shoulder, reminding you that your journey isn't finished.

"He who began a good work in you will carry it on..."

Those words matter. They speak right into every fear that whispers you're behind, every doubt that tells you you're not enough, every moment you wonder whether you're growing fast enough or doing things right. They remind you that God isn't just watching your life from far away. He is shaping it. Guiding it. Holding it. And He doesn't stop in the middle of the process.

Young athletes often feel pressure to reach the next level, figure out the next step, or prove they're improving. You may feel that pressure in your sport, but you may also feel it in your faith: wondering why you still struggle with certain things, why you still get anxious, why confidence fades, or why change takes longer than you hoped.

This verse shows you something important: God isn't disappointed by your pace. He's committed to your growth.

The work He started in you wasn't small. It wasn't accidental. It wasn't temporary. When He began shaping your heart, He did it with full intention. He knew what challenges you'd face. He knew the moments of discouragement that would shake you. He knew the victories that would lift you. He knew the days you'd trust Him with confidence and the days you'd trust Him with trembling hands.

Through all of it, He never stepped away.

Sometimes you only notice growth when you look back. At the start of the year, maybe you battled fears you now handle with more calm. Maybe you carried pressure that doesn't pull so hard anymore. At some point, you might have questioned whether God cared about the details of your life, but this year you've seen Him show up in quiet, personal ways, in conversations, in timing, in peace that arrived out of nowhere, in strength that didn't come from you.

Growth is often slow, but slow growth is still real growth.

Philippians 1:6 tells you that God Himself finishes what He starts. You are not responsible for perfecting your own heart. You're not the one carrying the weight of fixing everything inside you. Your job is to stay open, stay willing, stay close. God does the deep work. And He never leaves His work unfinished.

Think about how a coach invests in an athlete. A good coach doesn't quit halfway through the season. He doesn't walk away when the athlete struggles or hesitates. He keeps teaching, correcting, guiding, encouraging. He sees the bigger picture even when the athlete only sees one tough moment.

God is far more faithful than any coach. When He looks at you, He sees who you are becoming. He sees the strength He's building in you. He sees the character forming in the places that felt weak before. He sees the patience growing in seasons you didn't enjoy. He sees the courage rising where fear used to sit. He sees the heart that's learning to trust Him even when the path looks confusing.

You may think you've had unproductive weeks or wasted months. God doesn't see it that way. He sees the full arc of your story. He knows how each moment fits into the process of shaping your life. Nothing is lost with Him.

"He will carry it on..."

Not you alone.

Not your willpower alone.

Not your achievements alone.

He carries the work.

He strengthens the places where you feel fragile.

He gives clarity when your thoughts feel cloudy.

He lifts you when you feel drained.

He stays patient when you fall back into old habits.

He refuses to give up on you.

This verse is more than comfort. It tells you how to step into the next season of your life with trust, not fear. You don't need to pressure yourself to become something overnight. You don't need to worry that you'll mess up God's plan by taking a wrong turn. You don't need to fear being left behind.

You walk with a God who finishes what He begins.

As you move beyond these pages, remember that spiritual growth doesn't happen only in quiet moments. It happens on fields, on courts, in classrooms, at home, in the middle of long days and long seasons. God works in real life: the messy, loud, beautiful, difficult, surprising parts of it.

You will still have days when you feel uncertain. You will still have days when things don't go your way. You will still face pressure, mistakes, and moments where confidence dips. But now you know the truth: your growth isn't carried by your emotions. It's carried by God Himself.

He isn't done with you.

Picture Him walking beside you into a new year, reminding you gently, "I'm still working. I'm not finished. You are in My hands."

That's why this verse makes such a strong ending. It's not the end at all. It's the start of yet another chapter in your spiritual growth, where you'll see God's faithfulness in ways you didn't expect.

Before you close this devotion, place your hand over your heart for a moment. Breathe slowly. Let this truth rest inside you:

"God began a good work in me. And He will carry it on."

You don't walk into the next season alone.

You walk with the One who guides, strengthens, shapes, and completes.

He started something in you, and He will finish it with care.

God's work in you continues tomorrow, and the day after that, and every day to come.

Conclusion: Keep Growing, Keep Trusting, Keep Showing Up

As you reach the end of these fifty-two devotions, take a moment to breathe and notice where you are, not where you hoped to be, not where you fear you should be, but where you stand right now.

Finishing this book is more than checking off a goal. It means you've spent time each week turning your heart toward God, letting Him shape you in ways that go far beyond your sport.

Maybe some chapters met you in a heavy place. Maybe others encouraged you at just the right time. Maybe a few stretched you more than you expected. Growth rarely happens all at once. It happens in steady steps, honest moments, tough days, and quiet victories no one else sees.

If there is one thing I hope you carry with you, it is this: **you do not walk your path alone.** Not during practice. Not during games. Not in the car rides home. Not during the long weeks of school. Not in the moments when pressure rises or confidence slips. God is with you, not just as a distant idea, but as a present help, a steady guide, a loving Father who cares about every detail of your life.

Your sport will give you highs and lows, wins and losses, cheers and silence, but the deeper victory is learning how to stay grounded in God through it all. That's the kind of strength that lasts. That's the kind of foundation that carries you long after the season ends.

You don't have to be perfect to honor God.

You don't have to always feel brave.

You don't have to pretend you're not struggling.

You simply have to keep showing up. Showing up with an open heart, showing up with honesty, showing up with the willingness to trust God even when the way forward feels unclear.

As you move into your next season, whatever it looks like, remember the truths that have shaped this journey:

You are loved more deeply than you understand.

You are called to walk with courage, not fear.

You are strengthened by God, even when you feel weak.

You are guided by His wisdom, not by pressure or fear.

You are never forgotten, never overlooked, never on your own.

Your sport can help you grow in discipline, confidence, grit, and endurance. Your faith is what gives your life depth, meaning, and direction. When the two come together, your training and your trust, you become a different kind of athlete. One whose strength comes not only from muscles or technique, but from a heart anchored in God.

If at any point you need to start again, do it. God never tires of meeting you. If you go through a tough stretch, return to the verses that steadied you this year.

If fear rises, speak truth over it. If pressure builds, breathe and pray. If joy comes, thank Him for it.

Every moment, big or small, becomes a space where God can work in you.

My hope is that long after these devotions fade into your memory, the habits you built with them remain: turning to God first, trusting Him with each day, resting when you're weary, leaning on His strength, loving others well, and remembering who you are because of who He is.

You are an athlete, yes, but you are also God's child. That identity goes with you everywhere.

So, step forward with courage, with humility, with grit, and with faith that grows a little more each day. There will be challenges ahead, but there will also be moments of joy, breakthrough, and new strength. God will be there in all of it.

Let this truth stay close to your heart:

The God who began a good work in you will carry it through.

He isn't finished. And neither are you.

Keep growing.

Keep trusting.

Keep showing up.

God walks every step with you.

Reader Challenge:
Step Into the Year With Purpose

You've reached the end of this book, but you haven't reached the end of your growth. In fact, this is where things become real. Reading a devotional is one thing. Living it out, day after day, practice after practice, game after game, is something entirely different.

So, here is your challenge.

Take what you've learned this year and carry it into the spaces where it matters most. Into the moments when your legs burn, when your heart pounds, when pressure rises, when frustration hits, and when you wonder if you can keep going.

Bring it into the quiet places too: your room at night, a long bus ride, a break between classes, a walk after practice. These are the moments when faith becomes steady and real.

Choose one truth from these devotions that stuck with you. Maybe it was about trust or courage. Maybe forgiveness or stillness. Hold onto it. Let it shape the way you think, the way you play, and the way you treat people. Let it guide you through the tough days and lift you on the good ones.

Your challenge is not to be perfect this year. It's to stay open to God's voice. To keep inviting Him into your sport and your life. To ask Him for strength when you feel tired. To ask Him for peace when your thoughts feel crowded. To ask Him for courage when you doubt yourself, and to thank Him often for the way He meets you right where you are.

Every week, take one small step toward becoming the athlete, and the person God is shaping you to be. Some steps will feel big. Others will feel small. All of them matter. Growth rarely shouts. Most of the time, it whispers.

The world around you will tell you to earn your place. To keep proving yourself. To push harder every moment.

God invites you into something deeper. He invites you to walk with Him. To lean on Him. To trust Him. To grow in ways that go beyond a scoreboard, but also show up in how you play.

Let this be the year you go all in with Him.

Let this be the year you train your heart as intentionally as you train your body.

Let this be the year when faith becomes your calm, your courage, your anchor.

Always remember, God is with you in every step, every sprint, every breath. You are never alone: not in the quiet moments, not in the loud ones, not in the victories, and not in the losses. He walks with you, strengthens you, and guides you as only He can.

So, step forward. Step boldly. Step with intention. Let this be a year of growth, not just in your sport, but in your soul.

Your challenge begins now. God is with you all the way.

Closing Prayer

Lord,

Thank You for every page of this year, every lesson, every moment of growth, and every time You met me when I felt unsure.

Thank You for the strength You gave on hard days and the peace You brought when my heart felt crowded.

Thank You for the reminders that I am never alone, not in practices, not in games, not in school, and not in the quiet moments no one else sees.

As I step forward, guide me.

Shape my thoughts.

Steady my heart.

Help me play with courage, work with joy, lead with humility, and treat others with kindness. Let my sport be a place where Your character shows through me, whether I win or lose, whether the day feels light or heavy.

Teach me to trust You with my whole heart.

Teach me to rest when I am tired.

Teach me to listen for Your voice.

Teach me to follow Your ways even when the path feels unclear.

Protect my mind from fear, comparison, and pressure.

Fill me with faith that grows deeper than emotion.

Give me the strength to keep showing up, the patience to grow, and the bravery to live out what I've learned.

Thank You for loving me, leading me, and shaping me a little more each day.

I place this next season, every moment of it, into Your hands.

Amen.

Check out another book in the series

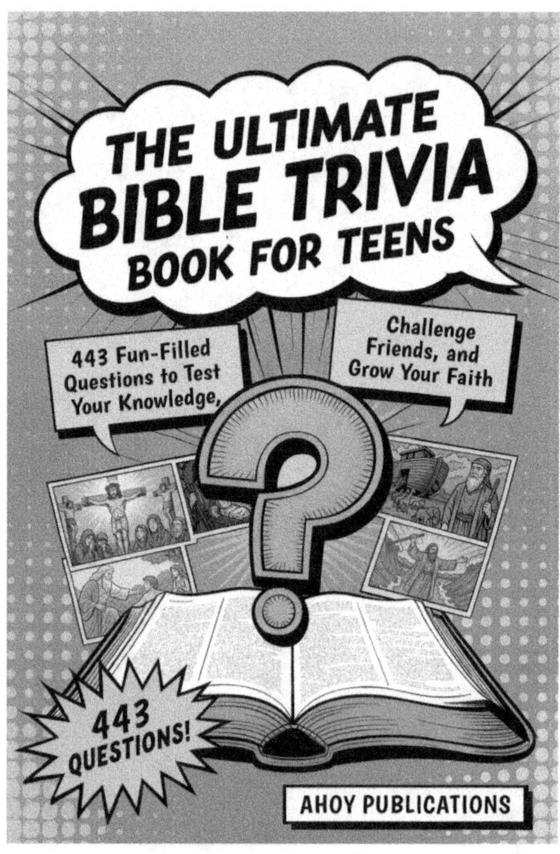

Welcome Aboard, Check Out This Limited-Time Free Bonus!

Ahoy, reader! Welcome to the Ahoy Publications family, and thanks for snagging a copy of this book! Since you've chosen to join us on this journey, we'd like to offer you something special.

Check out the link below for a FREE e-book filled with delightful facts about American History.

But that's not all - you'll also have access to our exclusive email list with even more free e-books and insider knowledge. Well, what are ye waiting for? Click the link below to join and set sail toward exciting adventures in American History.

Access your bonus here
https://ahoypublications.com/
Or, Scan the QR code!

www.ingramcontent.com/pod-product-compliance
Lightning Source LLC
Chambersburg PA
CBHW070854160726
48004CB00003B/1079